RETURN TO THE QUIET SELF

J. PRATAP

Made with ♥ on the Notion Press Platform
www.notionpress.com

There is a sacred strength in those who walk alone not out of rebellion, but out of reverence for truth.

This book is a tribute to the ones who feel deeply, love quietly, and carry ancient wisdom in their bones. The ones who have been called too sensitive, too intense, too much yet continue to choose authenticity over approval, solitude over noise, and presence over performance.

Return to the Quiet Self was born from countless soul-level conversations with strangers, seekers, and silent warriors who shared their stories not to be saved, but to be seen. In their words, I heard echoes of my own journey. In their solitude, I recognized a shared longing: to come home to ourselves.

This is not a manual. It is a mirror.
Not a roadmap, but a remembering.

For the Lone Wolf Empath.
For the Solophile.
For the cycle-breaker, the quiet leader, the one who walks softly but sees everything.

If you've ever felt like you don't quite belong, like your depth is a burden, or your silence misunderstood this is your space.
You are not broken. You are becoming.

This is your invitation to return not to who the world told you to be, but to who you've always been beneath the noise.

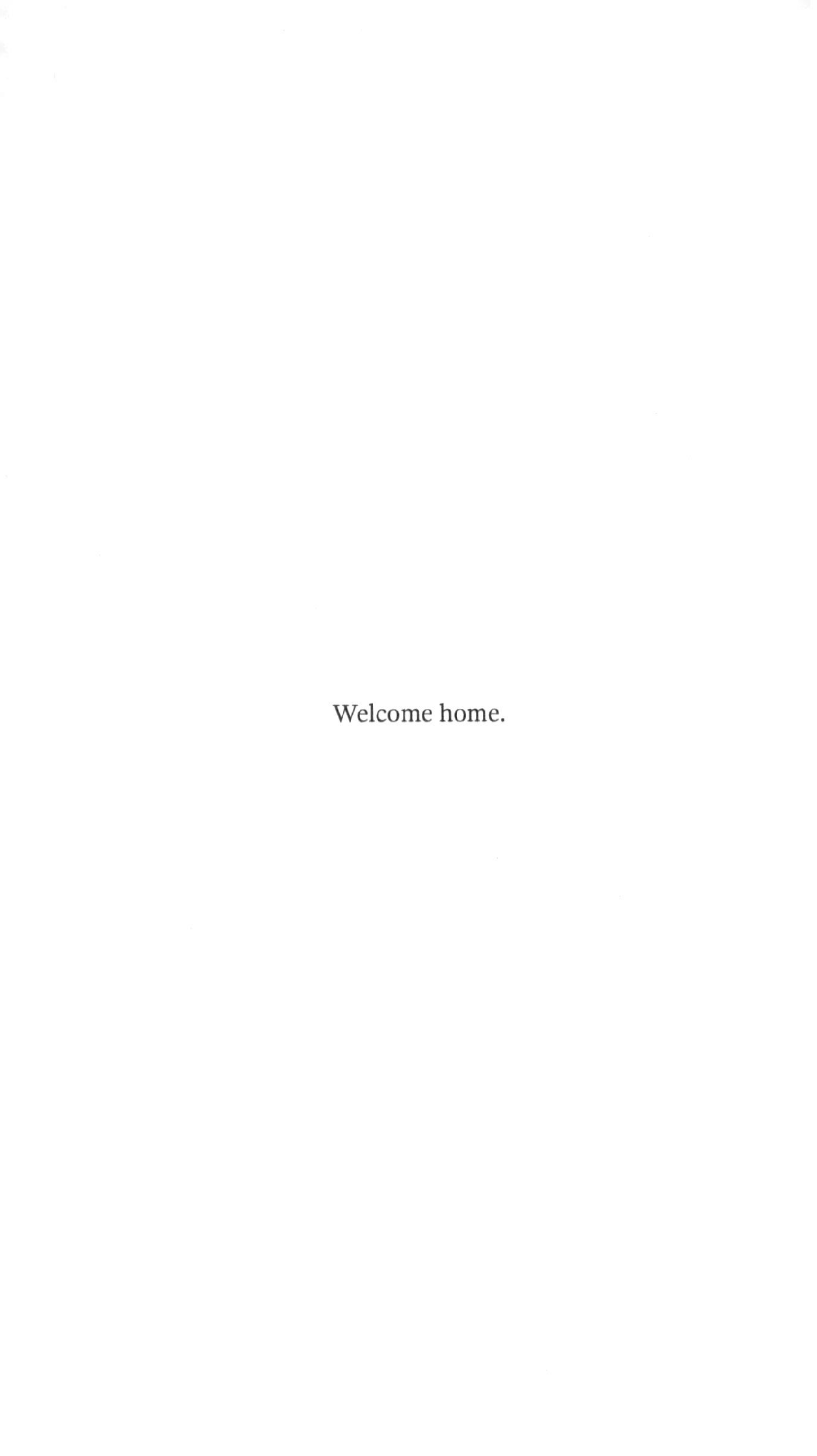

Welcome home.

Contents

Contents

Foreword

This book is not mine alone.

It was shaped by the voices of many people who, in moments of honesty and courage, shared their stories with me. Some were whispered in private messages. Others unfolded in long conversations, in passing comments, or in quiet confessions. Each one carried a thread of truth, a glimpse into the inner world of someone who had felt deeply, struggled silently, and longed to be seen.

Return to the Quiet Self is a reflection of those stories.

It is a tribute to the empaths, the introverts, the cycle-breakers, and the quiet souls who have walked through loneliness, burnout, and emotional overwhelm and still chose to keep their hearts open. It is for those who have felt like outsiders, not because they lacked something, but because they saw too much, felt too deeply, and refused to settle for surface-level living.

This book exists because of you.

Because you were brave enough to speak.

Because you trusted your truth.

Because you reminded me and now remind others that solitude can be sacred, and sensitivity is not a flaw, but a form of wisdom.

To everyone who shared a piece of their journey: thank you.

Your stories are woven into every page.

Your presence is felt in every word.

This book is for you.

And for anyone who has ever felt the same.

Preface

This book was not written in isolation.
It was shaped in the quiet spaces between conversations with strangers, friends, and kindred souls who trusted me with their stories.

Stories of feeling too much.
Of walking alone.
Of craving connection, but needing space.
Of choosing truth over approval, and solitude over noise.

Each story was a mirror. Each voice, a reminder that beneath our differences, there is a shared longing, to feel seen, to feel safe, to feel whole.

Return to the Quiet Self is not a guidebook or a solution. It's a reflection of those voices. A gathering of truths whispered by people who have lived through emotional overwhelm, spiritual awakening, and the quiet courage of choosing themselves.

This book is for them.
And for you if you've ever felt like your sensitivity was a burden, your solitude a flaw, or your depth too much for the world.

You are not alone.
You are not broken.
You are simply returning to the quiet, to the truth, to yourself.

Let this book be a companion on that journey.

Acknowledgements

I extend my deepest gratitude to all those who generously shared their stories, reflections, and lived experiences. Your openness and vulnerability have been instrumental in shaping the heart of this work.

To the quiet observers, the deep feelers, and those who walk their path with quiet strength this book is a reflection of your resilience and truth.

To those who offered support, encouragement, and space throughout this journey, your presence has been invaluable.

And to the reader thank you for your willingness to engage with these words. May they serve as a reminder that your story, too, holds meaning and power.

With sincere appreciation,

...

J. Pratap

Prologue

Return to the Quiet Self

There is a moment subtle, often silent when something within begins to stir.

Not because life is falling apart, but because it no longer feels aligned.

Despite outward success, a quiet ache lingers. A sense that something essential has been lost beneath the noise, the roles, the expectations.

This ache is not weakness. It is a signal.

A call to return not to the past, but to the self.

This book is for the Lone Wolf Empath the one who feels everything, yet often walks alone.

The one who seeks depth in a world of distraction, who chooses solitude not out of fear, but out of reverence for truth.

You are not broken. You are awakening.

The journey back to the quiet self is not easy. It asks you to let go of illusions, to sit with discomfort, to choose authenticity over approval, and presence over performance. It may feel lonely at times but it is not isolation. It is sovereignty. It is healing. It is homecoming.

You are not here to fit in. You are here to remember.

To reclaim your rhythm. To honor your sensitivity. To walk your own way home.

This is not a manual. It is a mirror.

A reflection of the path many have walked in silence.

A companion for those who are ready to return to the truth of who they are.

CHAPTER ONE

THE DESIRE TO BE LIKED

*The desire to be liked is the
beginning of surrender.*

The truth is,

The world doesn't care about your feelings.

It doesn't care if you want to be liked, or if you want everyone to think you're nice.

If you want to climb, to lead, to command, you have to understand this

power isn't polite.

Look around. Who really gets the respect? The man who begs for approval, softens every word, avoids conflict like the plague? Or the one who walks in calm, steady, with a quiet edge of danger beneath the surface the kind of presence that makes people stop talking and start thinking twice before crossing him?

I want you to imagine that man for a moment. He doesn't need to shout. His power whispers in the way he holds himself. His face never betrays panic, his voice carries no desperation. Even when chaos swirls around him, his hands don't tremble. That's what real strength looks like.

You see, the world is full of people who think power is about fangs, teeth, weapons raw force. But it's more than that. Fangs are symbols. They mark the line between those who act and those who wait for permission.

Here's the deal the man with fangs doesn't wait for the perfect moment. He creates the moment. He moves before conditions align, before the stars are in place. He understands something most don't

kindness without leverage is weakness.

Diplomacy without a hint of force is just noise.

Strength? It's not about destroying everything in your path. No, strength is choosing when not to destroy. It's holding back the power you have to show the world you're in control. The man who can ruin reputations but chooses not to is the one who really holds the cards.

Look closer. In politics, business, even personal relationships, this is how the game is played. The person who can walk away from the table sets the terms. The one who punishes betrayal without hesitation makes sure it doesn't happen twice. Power is spoken quietly, through action, not cries for sympathy.

I'm telling you this because if you want to lead, you must learn to be both steel and velvet. You must be soft in your voice but hard in your intent. Calm on the surface but capable of shaking the room if you choose.

Walk into a room and let them fear crossing you. Let them remember you not the whimper, but the fang. That's written into nature, into the instinct of men, into history itself. Those with teeth write the rules. Those without? They obey.

Want to know the first mistake most ambitious men make? They want to be liked. They chase affection like it's safety. They believe if everyone likes them, they'll be protected. But that's a lie.

The moment you put the approval of others above your own clarity, you hand over your power. You soften your actions, hesitate when you should strike. You calculate what's acceptable instead of what's necessary.

Here's the truth clarity demands decisions that will make you hated by many and respected by few. And hatred? Hatred isn't failure. It's a signal. It tells you that you're no longer furniture in other people's lives. That your presence matters. That you disrupt comfort.

Power cannot exist without enemies. Why? Because power creates a divide those above and those below. That divide breeds resentment, which breeds hatred. It's not a design flaw; it's the price you pay.

The weak crave affection because they believe it will shield them. They think if people like them, no one will strike. But approval is a fragile shield. It breaks the moment others' satisfaction fades. And when you must choose between what's right for you and what's comfortable for them, you will stand alone.

The strong don't fear that solitude. They accept it. They even calculate which hatreds are worth carrying. It's far better to be feared than loved, if you cannot be both. Love depends on fantasy and expectation one mistake and it's gone. But fear? Fear lingers. It keeps people in line long after affection fades. It silences betrayal, sharpens obedience. And when combined with respect, it builds unbreakable authority.

To be willing to be hated is to free yourself from the chains of public opinion. It means acting on your own terms. Moving without explaining. Punishing without apology. Speaking when others stay silent. Taking what others are too timid to reach for.

The people who change the world the rulers, the founders, the revolutionaries were hated by many in their time. Their names spat in the streets, whispered about behind closed doors, called evil by their enemies. But history doesn't ask if they were liked. It asks if they won.

If you try to be liked by everyone, you become harmless. You soften too much. You lose your voice. You disappear in compromise. You forget how to say no. You become a tool for others' will. And once you're no longer useful, you're discarded with the same polite smiles that once praised you.

Affection is a performance.
Stop acting, and the crowd moves on.
You have to decide what matters more?

The illusion of harmony or the reality of progress?

Real progress, in business, politics, and life, always comes at someone else's expense. You'll be called cruel for being efficient, arrogant for refusing to explain yourself, heartless for cutting ties. Let them talk. Their words are just noise the noise of people who never dared do what you are doing.

If you aren't hated by some, you aren't leading. You're following or standing still.

Hatred is the storm you walk through on the way up. It will come from below those who want your place. From beside you those who resent your pace. From above those who fear you may take their throne.

But if you stop walking because of the wind, you'll never see the view from the top.

Dominance is not soft. It's sharp. It's forged in discomfort and sustained by a refusal to be tamed.

The world doesn't reward the harmless. It silences them. Uses them. Forgets them.

You must reject weakness not just in the world, but inside yourself. The obedient dog must die so the wolf can rise a creature that doesn't beg, whimper, or wait for permission.

The wolf knows this

survival is not given. It's taken.

Others will seek virtue in submission. You, if you dare, become what they fear. Not for cruelty's sake, but for mastery. Not to destroy without cause, but never to be destroyed.

So listen carefully.

The path you want to walk isn't easy.

But it's yours if you choose it.

The question is do you?

CHAPTER TWO

THE GENTLE PRISON

A dog seeks approval to survive; a wolf demands respect to rule. One bows to fear, the other stands in power

It begins when men are told that to be good, they must be **agreeable.**

That to be noble, they must be **loyal.**

That to be worthy, they must be **obedient.**

And many believe it.

They fold themselves into the shape of what others need not because they are weak, but because they were never taught the price of being harmless.

They learn early that loyalty is praised that it earns approval, affection, a seat near power.

But few are told the truth

Loyalty is a currency. And the man who gives it freely becomes cheap.

He is celebrated when he submits, accepted when he yields, welcomed when he bends.

But make no mistake this is not virtue.

This is control.

A man shaped by the desire to be liked becomes predictable. His spine, slowly softened by years of quiet compromises. His instincts, blunted by the habit of asking permission. His voice, trained not to speak, but to be accepted.

He doesn't bark to warn.

He doesn't stand to protect.

He wags. He waits. He hopes.

Like a loyal creature who has forgotten it was once wild.

This is not the tragedy of a bad man this is the tragedy of a man taught to believe that self-erasure is goodness. That silence is safety. That kindness must cost you your edge.

But a man who cannot stand alone will never lead.

A man who fears rejection will never be respected.

He becomes the servant, the follower, the quiet shadow of stronger men.

And still he calls it virtue.

But virtue without discernment is a leash. And those who tighten that leash masters, ideologies, cultures rarely care if the one beneath it suffers. They care only that he obeys.

And when he stops obeying, they discard him without hesitation.

This is the danger of unconscious loyalty it is given as a gift, but received as an expectation.

You're praised for being useful until you are no longer useful.

You're honored for your service until you question your orders.

And once you do, the illusion cracks.

You were not loved.

You were tolerated.

You were not respected.

You were convenient.

This is not bitterness. This is clarity.

There is no nobility in being needed only when silent.

The world rewards those who walk with their eyes open those who offer their presence like a contract, not a sacrifice. Those who understand that real strength lies not in how much you give away, but in what you refuse to give for free.

The empath the one who sees, who senses, who feels the subtle tensions is especially vulnerable to this trap. Because they feel everything, they often trade their voice for peace. They offer loyalty, even when it is not returned. They stay, even when the room no longer deserves them.

But empathy without boundaries is a magnet for manipulation.

And kindness without clarity becomes complicity in your own diminishment.

You do not owe your silence to those who only value your obedience.

You do not owe your loyalty to people who use it as a shield for their own power.

You do not owe your gentleness to systems that punish strength disguised as quiet.

You were not born to live under the table, grateful for scraps.

You were not born to be the dependable shadow beside the throne.

You were not born to wag.

You were born to see. To choose. To stand.

Not recklessly. Not with noise.

But with clean intention and untouchable presence.

The world teaches you that to be feared is dangerous.

But it forgets to mention to be completely unfelt is worse.

The man who cannot command attention, who fears conflict more than erasure, will spend his life in the background of other people's victories.

True power is not about control.

It is about self-possession.

The quiet self does not need to be praised. It does not fear rejection. It does not perform for applause.

It watches. It discerns. It decides.

That is your return.

Not to rebellion. Not to cruelty. But to alignment.

To the understanding that kindness without strength is not virtue it is vulnerability.

That loyalty without wisdom is not devotion it is captivity.

That obedience without choice is not honor it is self-abandonment.

To be clear is not to be cruel.

To be grounded is not to be cold.

To walk alone is not to be lost.

It is to see with precision and choose with power.

That is where your real loyalty belongs.

To the quiet self.

CHAPTER THREE

THE CALL TO COME HOME

Lone Wolf Rising

Maybe you notice it late at night, lying awake and staring at the ceiling. Or maybe it sneaks up on you during a meeting, a party, or a casual conversation an invisible wave that washes over you, leaving behind a strange emptiness, a sense that what you're doing doesn't quite matter.

This feeling is the stirrings of your soul.

At first, you try to ignore it. You tell yourself it's just a rough patch, that you're tired or stressed. Maybe you think a vacation, a new hobby, or a fresh goal will shake it off. So you push it down, bury it beneath to-do lists, deadlines, and the noise of everyday life. But the whisper doesn't go away. It grows louder. More insistent. Harder to ignore.

Then one day, something inside breaks open.

Sometimes it's a big event heartbreak, loss, illness something that shakes your world. Sometimes it's nothing specific, just a sudden moment of stillness where everything you thought was true feels suddenly false. No fanfare, no warning just a deep, inescapable knowing that the life you've been living isn't really yours.

The walls you built start to crumble. The colors of your world shift. What once gave you comfort now feels hollow. What you chased with passion now feels meaningless.

This is the beginning of a spiritual awakening.

And trust me, no one is ever ready for it.

Spiritual awakenings don't come with a manual or a schedule. They don't wait for your permission. They storm through your life like a wild wind, tearing down the familiar so something new can grow. Your identity, your beliefs, your ambitions all the things you thought defined you begin to fall away.

It's terrifying.

It's confusing.

And yet, in the middle of that chaos, there's a strange kind of beauty.

Because beneath the noise and fear, something deeper is waking up.

A voice.

A presence.

A quiet knowing.

It's your soul. The part of you that's been buried under years of shoulds and musts. The part that's been calling you home, quietly but persistently.

Suddenly, the illusions you lived by the promises of success, money, fame, approval start to feel thin. Like paper cutouts instead of solid ground. You realize none of those things ever truly satisfied you. Not in the way your heart needed.

For the first time, you stop running.

You sit with the silence.

You let yourself feel the longing.

You grieve what you thought life was supposed to be.

This is the soul's cry for freedom.

And once you hear that cry, you can't un-hear it.

Some people try. They turn away, distract themselves with busyness or numbing habits. They retreat back into what's comfortable even if it hurts. Familiar pain feels safer than unknown freedom.

But for those who choose to listen, the journey ahead is sacred.

It's not an escape from life.

It's a return to it.

A return to what's real, what's true, what lasts.

The awakening draws you inward into the quiet corners of your heart, into the parts of yourself you forgot or never dared to see.

And slowly, almost without noticing, you start to change.

You speak more honestly to others and yourself.

You connect more deeply with people, with nature, with life.

You begin to see the beauty in small things you used to overlook: the way sunlight filters through leaves, the quiet sound of wind in the night, the still pause between breaths.

Life starts to feel like poetry not perfect, not always easy, but deeply meaningful.

Your pain becomes your teacher.

Your longing becomes your guide.

Yes, it gets lonely sometimes.

Few will truly understand what you're going through.

You may outgrow old friendships and question long-held beliefs.

The things that once excited you might lose their shine.

You will mourn who you were the version of you that didn't yet know.

But in letting go of the false, you make room for the real.

Awakening isn't about becoming someone new.

It's about remembering who you always were beneath the masks, beneath the noise.

It's about finding the sacred in everyday moments.

It's about living not from fear, but from love.

Not from performance, but from presence.

If you're reading this, and something inside you feels seen if there's a whisper in your heart saying, "Yes, this is me" then know this:

Your awakening is not a mistake.

It's not a breakdown.

It's not something to fix or run away from.

It's the beginning.

The soul has cried out.
And you've finally heard.
Welcome to the real journey.

CHAPTER FOUR

Too Much for the Pack

*How people Break Us, and Why Some
of Us Stay Broken Longer*

You don't become a Lone Wolf because it sounds poetic. You become one because the people who were supposed to love you first... didn't. Or couldn't. Or only did in pieces on the good days, in the right moods, under their terms.

One day, maybe quietly, maybe not you just realize you've been walking alone for years.

Through birthdays no one remembered. Through family dinners that felt more like performances than meals. Through Diwalis and New Years and Sunday afternoons where you sat in the same room as your people, but felt like a ghost no one could see.

You weren't raised by a pack.

You were raised by shadows.

By people who flickered in and out present in body, but somewhere far away in heart. They handed you duties, expectations, guilt... but rarely warmth. Rarely understanding. Rarely that safe, anchoring kind of love that tells a child: "You are seen. You matter. You are enough."

And in this land, the word family is sacred.

It's carved into wedding rituals. Chanted in prayers. Glorified in every movie, every festival, every speech from the elders. "Family is everything," they say. "Your family is your temple."

But what happens when the gods inside your temple don't look at you? When the ones who should have protected you handed you silence instead?

No, you don't become a Lone Wolf because it's noble.

You become one because staying in the pack was slowly erasing you.

Not all wolves howl. Some just... go quiet.

They stop speaking at the dinner table. They stop arguing when blamed. They nod even when misunderstood. In many Indian homes, silence isn't absence it's armor. It's the loudest language, passed down from parent to child like an unspoken manual: Don't speak too much. Don't feel too much. Don't need too much.

And from that silence, the Lone Wolf begins to take shape.

Not overnight. But slowly, in layers like mist creeping into a forest.

In birthdays skipped. In Rakhi threads tied more from habit than love. In comparisons that cut deeper than they were ever meant to. "Why can't you be more like your cousin?" or "Don't bring shame to the family." You hear those far more often than, "Are you okay?"

And so, the wolf is born not in some wild jungle but in living rooms filled with tension and traditions. In homes where the photo frames smile, but the people rarely do.

From the outside, it all looks fine.

You're at the weddings. You bow to the elders. You follow the script. But deep down, you know the truth: you're not part of a family. You're part of a performance. You're reading lines in a play you never auditioned for.

This is the Indian Lone Wolf's curse.

You're surrounded by people, yet raised by silence. You know all the family names and the rituals by heart, yet your heart rarely felt seen.

Here, we don't talk about emotional abandonment. We talk about obedience. About duty. About being "a good child." And if you ever step away? If you try to claim space for your truth?

You're suddenly ungrateful. You've become too modern. Too Western. Too much.

But let's be honest: the Lone Wolf didn't abandon the pack.

The pack abandoned them long before.

It happened when love came with conditions. When the only acceptable emotions were the ones that didn't make others uncomfortable. When needing love was seen as weakness. When expressing yourself was punished more harshly than staying quiet.

So you slip away. Not dramatically. Just... slowly. First emotionally. Then socially.

You become the one who doesn't visit home too often. The one who doesn't talk much. The one who celebrates their birthday alone and keeps their breakdowns even quieter.

At first, it feels like freedom.

You build your own space. You set your own rules. No judgment. No lectures. No pretending.

You light your own lamp for Diwali and convince yourself that peace is better than people. That solitude is strength.

But solitude has layers.

And when you peel them back, what you often find is not power but ache.

A quiet, persistent ache. The kind that shows up during festivals. That lingers when you hear others laugh around family tables. That makes you stare at your phone not expecting anyone to message, but still wondering why they don't.

People ask, "Why would anyone choose to be a Lone Wolf?"

The truth is: we didn't choose it. We adapted to it. We survived it.

Because some of us were never really included to begin with.

And here's the harder truth even when Lone Wolves find each other, it's not a fairytale.

Two people raised on silence, shame, and self-protection don't easily become a pack. They become mirrors. And sometimes, mirrors can feel like battlefields. Hurt people love cautiously. Trust slowly. Guard their scars like sacred relics.

And when two unhealed wolves try to love each other?

They might claw at each other, thinking they're holding hands.

This story goes deeper than just personal hurt. It's generational.

We inherit wounds here. Passed down like family heirlooms. Fathers who never said "I'm proud of you." Mothers who believed discipline was love. Grandparents who taught silence as strength. We didn't just inherit property and rituals we inherited stories half-told, traumas unspoken.

And some of us the more sensitive, the more neurodivergent we felt it harder.

The child who stared out the classroom window. The teenager who felt too much and said too little. The adult who craved real connection but couldn't tolerate superficial conversations.

We weren't defective. Just different. In a world that punished difference.

So we left the pack. Not to escape love but to escape distortion. To stop twisting ourselves into something more acceptable. To stop fighting for a kind of belonging that only ever came at the cost of our authenticity.

But leaving isn't the same as healing.

Distance gives space. But not always peace. Time gives perspective. But not always closure.

There comes a point in every Lone Wolf's life maybe in midlife, maybe after heartbreak, maybe just on a regular

Tuesday night where the silence becomes too loud.

And you begin to wonder...

Have I outgrown this armor?

Have I mistaken protection for isolation?

That's when the journey turns inward.

You stop blaming them not because they were right, but because you're tired of carrying their mistakes in your bones. You look at yourself the person built in the ruins of that family. And you ask: who am I without this pain? Without this defense?

You start to rewrite your story.

You don't need a new pack. You need a new truth.

One where asking for love isn't shameful. Where softness isn't punished. Where solitude isn't loneliness. Where being "different" isn't a flaw, but a gift.

And maybe just maybe someday, you meet another Lone Wolf.

Someone who's done their healing. Someone who isn't afraid of your shadows because they've made peace with their own. And you sit with them. Quietly.

No masks. No roles. No pretending.

Just presence.

Two wild hearts. Not untouched by fire but forged in it.

And in that stillness, for the first time in a long time...

you feel seen.

CHAPTER FIVE

WE'RE JUST BUILT FOR DEPTH.

*When I'm alone, I hear the things
I've been too distracted to notice*

When I'm alone, I hear the things I've been too distracted to notice the whisper of my intuition, the beat of my heart, the grief I've ignored, the dreams I almost gave up on.

Being alone is connection. Not with the world. With myself.

Most people run from solitude like it's a haunted house. They fill their days with noise, people, screens anything to avoid sitting in a room alone with their thoughts. Because silence doesn't lie. It reveals. And not everyone's ready to meet the truth living quietly inside them.

But me? I crave that silence.

I've come to learn that my solitude isn't a punishment it's my sanctuary.

The Lone Wolf… oh, they get misunderstood a lot. People call them cold. Distant. Emotionless.

But let me set the record straight.

Lone Wolves feel everything.

That's the problem.

They feel the static in a crowded room. The pain behind a fake smile. The shift in energy when someone's lying. They don't just see the world they *absorb* it. And when your spirit is that open, solitude becomes a form of survival.

It's not about avoiding the world.

It's about healing from it.

You know what's funny?

The world tells you to "find yourself," but it never tells you *where* to look.

Here's where I found me:

In empty cafes. In long walks without music. In solo dinners where I wasn't waiting for anyone to join me. In nights where the stars were my only company.

That's where I discovered I wasn't missing anything. I was just finally coming home.

People always ask: "Aren't you afraid of being alone?"

But maybe they should ask themselves: *"Why are you afraid to be?"*

Because the deeper truth is this every meaningful transformation starts in solitude.

The cocoon. The cave. The wilderness.

Jesus, Buddha, Moses whatever path you follow, it always begins with a walk into the unknown, into the silence, into the self.

Solitude isn't the absence of something.

It's the presence of everything that matters.

And yeah, I get it.

Some people thrive in groups, in parties, in loud spaces filled with laughter and glasses clinking. That's beautiful too.

But for those of us wired differently, who feel more at peace among trees than in crowds, whose favorite conversations are the ones we have with ourselves there's nothing wrong with that.

We're not broken. We're just built for depth.

I've met people who can't be alone for an hour. They panic in silence. They scroll their pain away.

And I've met others who've turned their solitude into art, poetry, healing, and strength.

Let me tell you something:

There's nothing more powerful than someone who chooses to stand alone and doesn't flinch.

Because in a world constantly telling you to be more, do more, connect more being still, being alone, being *enough* is the most rebellious thing you can do.

I've come to understand that aloneness isn't a state it's a **skill.**

A muscle.

A practice.

To sit with your own pain and not rush to cover it.

To celebrate your wins with no one watching.

To cry without a shoulder and still find the strength to get back up.

That's a rare kind of power.

You don't need an audience to validate your worth.

You don't need noise to feel alive.

You don't need a crowd to feel connected.

Because the deepest connection you'll ever feel is with your own soul.

And let's talk about the word "alone" for a second.

People hear "alone" and think "lonely," "outcast," "forgotten."

But break that word down, and what do you get?

All-one.

That's not isolation.

That's wholeness.

That's everything.

- So here's what being alone means to me:
- It means walking into a room and not shrinking.
- It means making choices without needing permission.
- It means building a life that makes sense to *me,* even if no one claps for it.
- It means not abandoning myself to be liked.
- It means hearing my own voice above the noise.
- It means answering to the mirror not the masses.
- It means having my own back, even when the world turns away.

Do people get intimidated by that?
Absolutely.

- Because people fear what they don't understand.
  And there's nothing more misunderstood than a soul that's *found itself.*
- I used to think I had to explain my aloneness.
  Now I realize: I don't owe that to anyone.
- Let them call it mysterious, or strange, or sad.
- Let them wonder how I do it.
- And I'll keep sipping my coffee in peace, smiling at the sky, rooted in a life that feels right for me.

So no, I'm not lonely.
I'm alone.
And that's exactly where I'm supposed to be.
Not lost. Not broken.
Just home.
With myself.
With the Earth.
With the quiet rhythm of my soul.
If that makes someone a Lone Wolf,
Then he'll wear that name like Kayo.
Because he've learned something the crowd hasn't

There's no greater power than knowing you are enough even when no one's looking.

CHAPTER SIX

THE EVOLUTION OF THE INNER LONE WOLF

How to Be a Lone Wolf in a Hyper-Social World

Let's begin with a controversial truth:

Social connection doesn't matter anymore.

Now, before you clutch your pearls, let me be clear this isn't a declaration against love, friendship, or community. It's a reframing of where true mental, emotional, and spiritual wellness originates: not outside of us, but within. In this chapter, we're not here to dismiss the value of others we're here to illuminate the radical importance of inner connection, especially for the Lone Wolf.

A Shift in the Pack Mentality

For decades, we've been sold on the idea that human beings need connection to survive and thrive. And in many ways, that's true for some. But what happens when the very connections we're told to pursue are laced with judgment, fear, and conformity?

What happens when socializing starts to feel like a performance, a mask you have to wear to be accepted? When you're surrounded by people, yet still feel completely unseen?

This is the burden the Lone Wolf often carries the pressure to belong, when everything inside them whispers: You already do. You belong to yourself.

The Inner World: A Forgotten Sanctuary

As children, we're taught to look outward for approval, for permission, for love. Few of us are shown how to cultivate a rich, nourishing relationship with our inner self that quiet, wise part of us that knows exactly who we are and what we need.

I didn't always understand this myself. Like many of you, I tried to "do the right thing." I joined teams. I worked in offices. I hosted dinner parties. I parented in public. I smiled and nodded in all the right places. And yet, despite the applause, I felt like I was betraying a deeper part of myself the one who just wanted to be alone. Not in sadness. Not in exile. But in sovereignty.

Solitude is Not a Symptom

In a world addicted to noise and distraction, solitude is often mistaken for sickness. "You must be depressed." "Are you okay?" "Why are you so distant?"

But the Lone Wolf knows: Solitude is not punishment it's a homecoming.

You don't become more of yourself by being around more people. You become more of yourself by spending time in your own energy, listening to your own voice, and building a relationship with the only person you'll be with for your entire life: you.

Breaking Free from the "Connection Myth"

One of the most dangerous lies we're fed is that without connection, we wither. But here's the truth: without inner connection, we crumble.

Yes, we need connection but not at the expense of our authenticity. Not the kind of connection that drains you, molds you, or forces you to perform in order to be seen.

In fact, most people don't know how to connect because they've never been taught how to connect with themselves. They chase relationships hoping to be filled, validated, or rescued. And when you, as a Lone Wolf, don't play that game, they misunderstand you. They call you avoidant. Distant. Cold.

But you're not cold. You're clear.

Choosing Inner Connection Over Outer Conformity

It takes courage to walk away from a room full of people and say, "I'd rather sit with myself."

It takes even more courage to reject the pack mentality and say, "Your path isn't mine."

When I left the traditional workforce, the dance teams, the motherhood cliques, and stepped fully into the unknown, people were quick to warn me: "You need people." But what I really needed was permission to trust myself.

Turns out, I didn't need anyone else's permission.

I just needed my own.

The Well-Connected Inner World

As a Lone Wolf, your inner world becomes your sanctuary. It's where ideas blossom, where intuition sharpens, and where peace lives. You are not disconnected you are deeply connected, just not in the way the world measures it.

Instead of dozens of surface-level friendships, you have a handful of deep soul connections. Instead of validation, you seek resonance. Instead of fitting in, you choose to stand firmly in your truth.

Redefining Connection for the New Era

We are entering a new era where inner connection is becoming the real gold standard. Where people are finally realizing that connection without consciousness is just noise. And that being alone doesn't mean being lonely it means being free.

The Lone Wolf isn't anti-social. The Lone Wolf is pro-authenticity.

The Inner Revolution Has Begun

So how do you be a Lone Wolf in today's world? You evolve. You connect not outwardly for approval, but inwardly for truth. You become whole within yourself, so you no longer seek others to complete you.

You walk your path. You protect your peace. You tune in to your own rhythm and walk to the beat of your inner drum even if no one else can hear it.

Because this isn't about rebellion.
It's about returning.
To your inner voice.
To your power.
To yourself.

CHAPTER SEVEN

THE LONE WOLF EMPATH

*Leaving the world a little more
honest than they found it.*

Some people are born with a map no one else can read. They move through life guided by instincts too ancient to explain, drawn to silence like moths to the moon. These are the Lone Wolf Empaths quiet observers with wild hearts, wired to feel everything and yet belong nowhere. The world calls them distant, strange, even cold. But beneath that calm exterior lies a storm of emotion, sensitivity, and intuition too vast for the average life to hold. They are not broken. They are built differently. And in their difference lies a kind of magic the world desperately needs but rarely understands.

There are souls in this world who are born with rain in their eyes and fire in their bones. They do not move with the herd. They do not echo the voices of the crowd. They walk softly, but not out of fear only because they are listening to things most people cannot hear.

They are the Lone Wolf Empaths.

Misunderstood and mislabeled, they are not simply introverts, nor are they merely "sensitive people." No, these are the ones who can feel the sorrow of a room before anyone speaks. Who can read the shift in someone's energy before words betray the truth. They carry within them a radar for emotion, tuned so finely that the world often feels like a thunderstorm they have no umbrella for.

And so, they walk alone. Not out of pride.

Not out of bitterness.

But

because silence is the only place they can hear themselves think.

This is not a path of exile.

This is a path of survival.

1. *The Gentle War: Loneliness vs. Contentment*

To be a Lone Wolf Empath is to be caught in a constant inner tug-of-war a paradox where the soul longs to be held, even as the spirit begs for solitude. They crave connection, but not the shallow kind that passes for friendship in the modern world. They want soul-to-soul communion, and anything less exhausts them.

It's not uncommon for these empaths to withdraw after social events not because they didn't enjoy themselves, but because every conversation was another wave of emotional data crashing into them. A single dinner party can feel like running a marathon in someone else's shoes.

And so, they retreat.

Yet, here lies the contradiction: even in their treasured solitude, a ghost of loneliness lingers. It whispers late at night. It paces the walls of their mind during long walks. They wonder: Am I alone because I choose it or because no one truly sees me?

The world tells them they need people. That isolation is unnatural. But what if their aloneness isn't a wound but a medicine?

For the Lone Wolf Empath, contentment comes not from being around people, but from being around peace. Their sacred ratio might be 80% solitude, 20% connection and they must learn to honor that without shame. To stop apologizing for needing time alone. To stop labeling themselves "anti-social" or "too sensitive."

They are not broken.
They are built differently.
And that's okay.

2. The Mirror Trap: The Addiction to Highs and Hurts

There is a certain kind of pain that masquerades as love.

It begins beautifully. Intoxicating. Electric. Someone enters the empath's life like a lightning strike, offering words that feel like balm. They say, "I've never met anyone like you." And the empath, starved for understanding, opens the gates wide.

But this is how the trauma bond is born.

It is not love. It is a mirror trap an emotional bait-and-switch where initial idealization is followed by slow corrosion. The one who once admired them begins to criticize, control, and withdraw. The empath stays, not out of weakness, but out of a desperate hope that the "real" version the one who loved them might come back.

They confuse intensity with intimacy. And like an addict chasing the first high, they keep returning, hoping to feel whole again.

It's a cruel cycle: idealize, devalue, discard.

Worse still, Lone Wolf Empaths often internalize the discard. They believe they were too much. Too sensitive. Too intense. So they retreat not just from that person, but from life. They become wary, guarded, suspicious of anything that smells like connection.

What they don't realize at first is that the addiction isn't to the person. It's to the feeling of being seen.

To break this cycle, they must become their own witness. Their own mirror. Their own source of validation. They must detox from toxic people like recovering alcoholics, even when loneliness claws at their skin.

Because love that costs your self-worth is not love.

It's self-abandonment.

3. The Sacred Flame: Creativity as Survival

In the quiet aftermath of heartache, when the world has faded to gray, something else stirs in the empath's bones.

The need to create.

To write, to paint, to build, to dance somehow, expression becomes the oxygen they forgot they needed. Alone with their thoughts, the Lone Wolf Empath doesn't simply cope they transform.

They don't just tell stories.

They bleed them.

Their creativity is not a hobby. It's their second language. Their way of translating the chaos inside into something tangible. And in that act, they regain power. What once drowned them now becomes art. What once shamed them now becomes beauty.

But creativity, too, is fragile.

It suffers under the weight of emotional chaos. Toxic relationships dim the fire. Addictive bonds silence the muse. A single toxic connection can cost months of creative clarity.

That's why solitude isn't a luxury it's a requirement.

When their space is safe, when their heart is quiet, the Lone Wolf Empath can channel the wildest storms into stories. They can sculpt wounds into wisdom. They can turn silence into symphonies.

They don't need a stage.

They just need stillness.

4. A New Way to Walk the World

There is no manual for being a Lone Wolf Empath.

No rulebook. No map.

What works for others may never work for them. And this is the hardest part: trusting that their rhythm, their timing, their wild way of being is enough.

They don't lead in the traditional sense. They don't scream for attention or command a room. Their power is quieter. Subtler. It comes in the form of a single sentence that stays with you for years. A painting that stops time. A truth so honest, it makes people cry without knowing why.

They lead by existing fully. Authentically. Bravely.

They don't seek followers.

They just walk wild, uncontained, and true and others who are searching for something real begin to follow the footprints in the snow.

That is their leadership. That is their legacy.

Final Thoughts: The Strength in Solitude

The world may never fully understand the Lone Wolf Empath.

Their silence is too loud. Their truth is too raw. Their need for space is often mistaken for distance. But those who truly know them those who have seen their fire up close understand the gift they carry.

They are not broken. They are rare.

They walk the world with a compass most people don't even know they've lost.

And yes, their path is often lonely. But it is also luminous.

Because in choosing themselves, again and again, they light a torch for every other misfit, dreamer, and wanderer who thought they were walking alone.

They're not.

The Lone Wolf Empath was here.

Quietly. Powerfully.

Leaving the world a little more honest than they found it.

THE WISDOM OF THE LONE WOLF

Life is not a competition.

There's an old legend that begins this chapter, and it holds more truth than any modern self-help book ever could.

"A fight is going on inside me," the wise elder says to his grandson. "It's between two wolves. One is evil he's anger, envy, regret, greed, guilt, resentment. The other is good he's peace, joy, humility, kindness, compassion, and truth."

The boy asks, "Which wolf will win?"

"The one you feed," the elder replies.

And right there, in that one sentence, lies the entire secret to getting ahead of 99% of people.

The Hidden Fight Inside Us All

Most people spend their entire lives feeding the wrong wolf. Not because they are bad or weak, but because no one ever taught them any different. They feed the wolf of comparison, jealousy, fear, and doubt. They surround themselves with other wolves doing the same, and together, they stay stuck. Comfortable, but stuck. Fed, but starving.

The truth? **99% of people are trying to solve their internal emptiness by chasing external things** a fancier job, a bigger house, a better body, more followers, more love, more validation. They think if they just keep running, eventually they'll arrive at peace.

But you can't outrun the wolf inside you.

The Distraction Disguise

We live in a world full of distractions that wear the costume of purpose. Society sells us happiness, but only after you achieve this or buy that. Education, careers, relationships, even the pursuit of peace these can all become traps if you chase them to escape yourself.

It's not that these things are bad. It's that **99% of people chase them because they're afraid of being still.**

- Stillness means silence. And silence forces you to hear the voice inside the one that whispers the truth you're too scared to admit.
- So, what does the 1% do differently?
- They stop chasing.
- They stop feeding the wrong wolf.
- They become the Lone Wolf.

Redefining What It Means to Get Ahead

Let's get something straight: getting ahead doesn't mean being richer, more famous, or better looking than everyone else. That's just playing a louder version of the same game.

To truly get ahead of 99% of people, **you have to stop playing the game entirely.**

You have to walk your own path. Not because you want to be better than others, but because **you've realized the race has no finish line.**

Most people are sprinting in circles. The 1% is sitting on a mountain, watching the chaos below with calm eyes.

The Power of Being Alone

Here's the part that most people won't want to hear: the path to that mountain begins with **being alone.**

Not lonely.

Alone.

There's a huge difference.

Loneliness is what happens when you resist being alone. When you think something is missing.

But aloneness true, powerful solitude is what happens when you realize **nothing is missing.**

The Lone Wolf doesn't fear solitude. They embrace it. They use it to sharpen their senses, reflect on their thoughts, and reconnect with the inner self most people spend their lives avoiding.

Breaking Free From the Pack

The hardest thing you'll ever do is take your first step away from the pack. The pack is warm. It's familiar. You know your place in it even if that place doesn't feel right.

But staying with the pack means living in a constant state of comparison. Who's more successful? Who's happier? Who's more liked?

The Lone Wolf doesn't ask these questions. Not because they don't care, but because they **no longer need the answers.**

The Lone Wolf understands that their worth is not up for debate.

They are not running a race.

They are on a journey.

Turning Loneliness into Power

Science tells us that loneliness changes our brain. It makes us less trusting, more afraid, and more likely to isolate further. It becomes a self-reinforcing trap.

But here's the thing: loneliness doesn't come from being alone. **It comes from being disconnected from yourself.**

That's the real epidemic people who have no idea who they are when the noise stops. And so, they fill their lives with constant noise.

The Lone Wolf chooses silence.

Not because it's easy.

But because it's real.

Self-Connection Is Survival

In a world that teaches us to depend on everything outside of ourselves, the greatest act of rebellion is to **depend on yourself.**

Not in a selfish way. Not in an isolated way. But in a grounded, present, and powerful way.

When the Lone Wolf fails, they don't blame others they learn.

When the Lone Wolf is hurt, they don't seek revenge they reflect.

When the Lone Wolf is alone, they don't feel empty they feel full.

This is the kind of strength that the 99% may never understand. Because the pack teaches you that your strength lies in numbers. The Lone Wolf knows that real strength lies in **self-mastery**.

The Gift of Stillness

Here's something no one tells you: **you already have everything you need.**

The reason most people never discover this is because they never stop moving long enough to notice it. They're sprinting through life, jumping from goal to goal, hoping that the next thing will finally make them feel complete.

The Lone Wolf knows that completion isn't something you find. It's something you **remember.**

When you stop looking outward and turn inward, you find a peace that no amount of success, love, or validation can offer.

You discover the wolf you've always been meant to feed.

Living For Yourself, Not Against Others

The 1% understands something vital: **life is not a competition**.

You're not here to outdo anyone.

You're not here to win.

You're here to **wake up**.

To realize that your purpose isn't about achieving something extraordinary, but about remembering that you already are.

One Final Truth

The difference between the Lone Wolf and the pack is not about arrogance or superiority. It's about **authenticity**.

The Lone Wolf doesn't pretend to fit in.

They don't chase validation.

They don't shape-shift to make others comfortable.

They accept that they are different. And instead of fighting it, they **honor it**.

And that's the secret.

That's how you get ahead of 99% of people.

You stop trying to get ahead at all.

You stop running.

You start being.

The Challenge For You

- So here's the question only you can answer: **Which wolf will you feed?**
- Because the one you feed becomes the one you follow.
- And the one you follow decides your path.
- The pack might feel safer, but it will never set you free.
- Only the Lone Wolf walks the path of truth. Of stillness. Of presence.
- And if you're still reading this... maybe that Lone Wolf has been waiting inside you all along.
- Don't wait any longer.
- **Set it free.**

CHAPTER NINE

RIGHT PEOPLE, FEWER DISTRACTIONS

Your sensitivity isn't a flaw it's fuel.

They don't talk about people like you.

Not in the glossy self-help books. Not in the trending podcast episodes. Not in the way that feels real.

You've always known you're different but not in a way that screams for attention. You feel things deeper than most. You notice too much. You carry people's moods like storm clouds in your chest. And while others thrive in the noise of the world, you crave silence like it's oxygen.

But silence can be sharp, too. Silence makes you confront things you've been trying to outrun like loneliness, grief, or the ghosts of people you've loved too hard.

You're not just an empath.

You're a Lone Wolf empath wired for solitude, but starving for meaning. Craving connection, yet allergic to chaos. A walking contradiction that no one really understands.

This chapter is for you.

1. Loneliness vs. Contentment: The War Inside

There's a particular kind of ache that lives in the Lone Wolf empath: a pull between wanting to be left the hell alone and wanting someone to see you really see you and stay.

On the outside, it looks like introversion. But it's not that simple.

You need people... but only the right ones. And the right ones? They're rare.

Most social interactions drain you. Small talk feels like emotional theft. Crowds make your skin itch. You leave dinner parties with headaches, and text messages from certain people can ruin your entire day.

But when you're alone too long, something else creeps in: that sharp edge of loneliness. Not boredom something heavier. The kind that makes you question whether you've cut off too much, whether solitude has turned into self-sabotage.

And that's the core of the Lone Wolf empath's first struggle: you're constantly toggling between freedom and isolation.

You've let go of the draining friendships. You've walked away from the people who only took, never gave. And you're better for it. But the silence they leave behind? That part stings more than you admit.

Eventually, you learn that this inner war isn't something to "fix" it's something to understand. You begin to notice your own rhythm: maybe 80% solitude, 20% deep, intentional connection. Not the shallow stuff. Not the text-back-in-5-minutes expectations. You need soul-level connection or nothing at all.

That's not antisocial. That's honest.

2. The Addiction No One Talks About: People as a Drug

Let's talk about the cycle you've probably lived a dozen times, even if you don't have the words for it yet.

You meet someone. They come in hot obsessed with your depth, your sensitivity, your "vibe." You feel seen. Finally. For once, you think, Maybe I don't have to do this life thing alone.

And then, it flips.

The admiration turns to criticism. The connection becomes control. Suddenly, you're walking on eggshells, trying to get back to the version of them that made you feel alive.

But they're gone.

What's left is the emotional whiplash of the trauma bond: that painful loop of idealization, devaluation, and abandonment. They hooked you on a version of themselves that never really existed, and now you're stuck chasing a high that only hurts you.

Sound familiar?

That's not love. That's addiction.

Lone Wolf empaths are especially vulnerable here. When you're starving for real connection, you're easy prey for people who offer intensity instead of intimacy. They flood your nervous system with adrenaline, call you their soulmate, then vanish or worse, stay and rot you from the inside.

And here's the twisted part: the drama can feel addictive. It gives your loneliness something to do. It tricks your brain into thinking you're alive, even as it drains your soul.

But the crash always comes. Every time.

Getting out of that loop isn't just about cutting them off. It's about sitting in the withdrawal the nights that feel empty, the days you question your worth, the temptation to go back.

This is where you either break the cycle... or repeat it.

And breaking it means building a new kind of connection. One with yourself. One that doesn't require chaos to feel real.

3. The Wild Gift: Creativity as Salvation

Here's the part no one talks about enough: your sensitivity isn't a flaw it's fuel.

When you're not tangled in toxic relationships or over-explaining your feelings to people who don't care, you create.

Art. Music. Writing. Photography. Dreaming. Whatever your medium is, creativity is where your soul exhales.

When you're alone, when you're centered, your mind opens up. You hit that sacred space called flow, where time disappears and something bigger moves through you.

This is where the Lone Wolf empath becomes a force.

But the catch? If your life is too chaotic if you're stuck in addiction cycles, surrounded by the wrong people, or constantly trying to "fix" relationships you lose access to it. Your creativity short-circuits. Your mind clogs with emotional debris.

In that sense, protecting your energy isn't just a mental health thing it's a creative survival strategy.

When you're in alignment, you produce beauty that speaks to people's souls. You're not just making things you're transmitting something sacred. That's your gift. That's your power.

And it only thrives when you guard your solitude like a fortress.

So, What Now?

Here's the hard truth: being a Lone Wolf empath means walking a path that won't always make sense to other people. You'll be misunderstood. Judged. Told you're "too much" or "too distant" or "too sensitive."

Let them talk.

You're not here to please people. You're here to feel, to create, to heal, and to build a life that doesn't burn you out.

The next time you feel that tug that ache to text someone toxic, that guilt about spending another weekend alone, that inner critic whispering that you're broken pause.

Ask yourself:

- Am I lonely? Or am I just detoxing from unhealthy connection?

- Is this person nourishing my soul, or just filling the silence?

- Am I betraying myself to avoid a feeling that will pass?

Because the truth is, you don't need more people.

You need the right people, fewer distractions, and more trust in your own rhythm.

And once you embrace that? The loneliness softens. The creativity returns. The self-love gets loud.

You don't become harder. You just become wiser.

CHAPTER TEN

THE LOVE DILEMMA

You are not too much. You were just giving it to those who could only love halfway.

To the world, they appear composed self-sufficient, maybe even aloof but beneath that calm surface stirs a storm of emotion, sensitivity, and longing that doesn't quite know where to land.

Love, for them, isn't just an emotion it's an experience of energy, alignment, and presence. But why, then, is it so difficult?

Let's begin with a truth many lone wolf empaths don't say out loud: they've never really fit into the traditional ideas of love. Not because they don't want to, but because those boxes were never made for them.

They don't just walk alone they love alone, too.

Most people follow a map when it comes to love: date, fall, marry, settle, repeat. But the lone wolf empath? They create their own path, often stumbling through forests no one else dares to enter, carrying an odd mix of independence and empathy. It's not rebellion for rebellion's sake. It's instinct. Conformity dulls their light. And when they've tried to wear masks or shrink into molds, love has slipped right through their fingers.

They are not cold. Far from it. Their hearts beat fiercely. But they've learned sometimes too early, sometimes too harshly that love, when unguarded, can wound. Deeply.

So over time, a wall goes up. Not to keep love out, but to stop the wrong kind of love from getting in.

The struggle, at its core, is energetic.

You see, within every lone wolf empath exists a delicate dance between the masculine and the feminine. Not man and woman but energy. The masculine shows up as strength, independence, structure. The feminine as intuition, empathy, and flow. Most people live lopsided too much in one, too little of the other. But the lone wolf empath balances both. That's their gift and their curse.

When these energies aren't harmonized, love becomes lopsided too. Either they love too much and lose themselves... or they love too little and lose the chance. They retreat. They return. They give too much. Then they vanish. Because loving with a wide-open heart while carrying the weight of past wounds is like dancing barefoot on broken glass.

Still, they try.

Let's talk about trauma not as a buzzword, but as a blueprint.

Many lone wolf empaths carry invisible scars from childhood. Love may not have been modeled well. "I love you" might've been rare or conditional. Affection may have come with expectations, punishment, or silence. And so, from an early age, the empath learns to question love. To chase it. To hide from it. To recreate it with people who cannot give it.

They begin to believe that love means fixing someone. Or saving them. Or sacrificing themselves entirely to earn affection.

This isn't compassion. This is trauma playing dress-up.

Let's break it down simply:

1. **Hyper-independence** becomes a shield.
   They say, "I don't need anyone," but deep down, they're terrified of needing someone who won't stay. They'd rather build a fortress than risk another betrayal.
2. **Fear of being misunderstood** lingers.
   Their depth can't be translated easily. They feel different because they are. In love, this creates distance. They either over-explain or go silent. Either way, they're not truly seen.

3. **Overgiving and burnout** follow.
   They pour and pour and pour... until there's nothing left. Then comes the resentment. Then the retreat. The silence. The reboot.

It's a painful cycle one that leaves them wondering if love is worth it at all.

But here's what's beautiful: through the chaos, the lone wolf empath evolves. Slowly. Painfully. Honestly.

They begin to realize that their gift isn't in changing people, it's in holding space for themselves. They no longer mistake pity for love, or attachment for loyalty. They stop rescuing lovers and start rescuing their own soul.

Because eventually, they understand:

Love is not sacrifice. Love is alignment.

And so, the healing begins.

There's an old quote that says:

"Imagine being loved the way you love."

That thought alone brings tears to many lone wolves' eyes. Because their love is deep, pure, attentive. They remember small details. They feel what others don't say. They hold people's wounds like sacred secrets. But they've rarely received the same in return.

Why?

Because most people don't meet them at the same frequency. Not because they're better just different. And difference, when not understood, becomes isolation.

But here's the secret the lone wolf empath eventually learns:

You don't need to be loved by everyone. You only need to be seen by someone.

Balance is the key.

The wounded feminine says, "I'll give anything to be loved."

The healed feminine says, "I'll love without losing myself."

The wounded masculine says, "I'll never need anyone again."

The healed masculine says, "I am strong enough to be vulnerable."

And in that balance between surrender and strength, solitude and connection the lone wolf empath discovers a different kind of love. Not romantic. Not dramatic. But sacred.

They begin to attract lovers who are not projects. Who do not drain them. Who do not need saving.

Instead, they attract mirrors.

Someone who dances with them, not around them.

And still, even in healing, there is grief.

Grief for the years spent loving the wrong people.

Grief for the self-abandonment.

Grief for the "almosts," the "could've beens," the "maybe next times."

Grief for the belief that love required effort, endurance, or pain.

But after the grief comes clarity.

The lone wolf empath stops chasing. Stops explaining. Stops shrinking.

They don't want textbook love anymore.

They want presence.

They want energy that matches theirs without performance.

They want the kind of silence that feels full, not awkward.

They want a partner who asks, "How's your heart today?" instead of "What's wrong with you?"

Love, they realize, is not about finding someone to complete them.

They were never incomplete.

Love is about meeting someone who respects your wholeness and still wants to learn you every day. Slowly. Quietly. Eternally curious.

And when that kind of love shows up, the lone wolf empath doesn't feel the need to run.

Because finally, it doesn't feel like sacrifice.

It feels like home.

In the end, the lone wolf empath understands this simple truth:

You are not too much. You were just giving it to those who could only love halfway.

So they sit quietly, in their cave of self-knowing, no longer waiting for someone to light the fire.

They've already learned to do it themselves.

And maybe, just maybe, someone will sit beside that fire someday

Not to warm themselves...

But to share in the glow.

CHAPTER ELEVEN

HOW TRAUMA CHANGES OUR NEED FOR CONNECTION

Not all of us are tuned to the same frequency

From the moment we are born, our biology tells us to connect. A newborn cries out, not just for food or warmth, but for touch for the soothing voice of a caregiver, for the comfort of being held. It's said that we are hardwired for connection, that survival depends on it. And for many, that's true.

But what happens when connection is where the pain began?

What happens when the people we were supposed to trust those who were meant to nourish and protect us became the very source of our fear, our betrayal, our trauma?

For some of us, connection doesn't feel safe. It feels like danger.

According to neuroscience, our brains are wired to crave belonging. Loneliness is treated like an alarm system, a signal that something vital is missing just like thirst signals dehydration, or hunger signals an empty stomach. But that assumes one crucial thing: that everyone's brain is receiving those signals in the same way.

The truth is, not all of us are tuned to the same frequency.

Some people walk through the world barely noticing the ache of loneliness. Others don't even recognize it when it shows up. They'll tell you, "I'm fine being alone. I never get lonely." And they mean it. Because for them, solitude is not a void it's a sanctuary. It's not something they settled for; it's something they chose, even if they had to choose it because their nervous system demanded it.

This isn't just a personality trait. Often, it's a wound. A wound stitched into the nervous system by years of hypervigilance, betrayal, abandonment, or simply growing up in an environment that taught them people can't be trusted. And when that kind of trauma takes root early, it doesn't just change how we feel about connection it changes how we need it.

Imagine you're someone who flinched at every raised voice, who read a hundred unspoken cues to survive dinner, who learned not to cry too loud or ask for too much. Now imagine someone tells you, "You just need more friends. You need to socialize. That'll help."

It's like handing water to someone who's forgotten how to drink.

We're told that humans are pack animals. That we're made to live in tribes. That community is key. But for those of us whose "tribes" once felt like battlegrounds, that message becomes complicated.

Some of us crave connection, but don't trust it.

Some of us seek intimacy, but flinch at touch.

Some of us want to be seen, but are terrified of being truly known.

And then there are those of us who've adapted so well to solitude that anything else feels foreign. We've learned how to fill our own cups, to regulate our own emotions, to rely on the forest more than a friend, to find peace not in parties but in the pages of a book or the stillness of the sky.

That doesn't mean we're broken.

It means we've evolved differently.

Trauma doesn't just leave emotional scars. It rewires the brain. It recalibrates the nervous system. It teaches us to scan every room for threat, to prepare for the worst, to hold our breath even when everything seems fine. And in that kind of body, connection can feel like a risk. Sometimes, even love feels dangerous.

So what do we do?

We protect ourselves. We pull back. We build walls instead of bridges not because we don't want connection, but because connection has become a battlefield where we've lost too much.

And yet, here's the paradox: even those of us who avoid connection still carry the memory of needing it. There's a hunger there, buried deep beneath the layers of fear and self-reliance. It's just quieter. More selective. It doesn't cry out for a crowd. It yearns for something rare: safety. Presence. Realness.

When trauma survivors do connect, it's different. We don't want surface-level chatter. We want soul. We want eyes that don't lie. We want energy that feels calm, not chaotic. We're not interested in small talk we want depth. Honesty. Integrity. We want to feel someone's truth, not their mask.

And we're willing to be alone until we find that.

Some might call that being picky or antisocial. But it's not about rejection it's about protection. It's about knowing what your system can tolerate and refusing to betray yourself just to "fit in."

People talk about loneliness like it's a universal curse. But for some of us, it's more bearable than unsafe company. We've known the loneliness of being misunderstood in a crowd. Of being unseen in a relationship. Of being dismissed in a family. That kind of loneliness cuts deeper than solitude ever could.

For us, solitude becomes sacred.

It becomes a healing ground.

It's where we regulate, recharge, reconnect with ourselves, with nature, with a sense of peace that's hard to find in human noise.

Some of the most self-aware people you'll meet are those who've learned to be alone. They've walked into the dark parts of themselves without running. They've made friends with silence. They've confronted pain without distraction. And that kind of inner connection? It's powerful. It's grounding. It's rare.

So no, not everyone is wired for connection in the same way. Not everyone feels the social pull with the same intensity. And that's okay.

Neurodivergence plays a role too. For those who are autistic, highly sensitive, or otherwise neurologically unique, social interactions can be draining, confusing, even painful. The signals their brain sends aren't broken they're just different. And when the world keeps pushing one-size-fits-all advice about "getting out there" and "meeting people," it leaves them feeling alienated, misunderstood.

We need to update our understanding of connection.

Because sometimes connection doesn't look like coffee dates or group chats. Sometimes it looks like tending to plants, or whispering to animals, or sitting beneath a tree and feeling deeply held. Sometimes it looks like journaling, or painting, or meditating like creating a dialogue with the divine, the earth, or the quiet voice inside.

Sometimes, that is enough.

And other times, yes, we do long for people. But not just any people. We crave safe souls. Gentle energies. Relationships that don't demand we abandon our boundaries. Friendships where silence isn't awkward, but welcomed. Partnerships built on mutual respect, not performance.

As we heal, our connection needs evolve.

We no longer look for people to fix us or fill the void. We've learned to be with ourselves in our worst moments, so we're not looking for saviors. We're looking for companions. Mirrors. Kindred spirits.

Healing also teaches us something radical: we don't have to explain or justify our solitude. We don't have to feel guilty for needing less than others. We don't have to keep trying to be someone we're not just to be accepted.

There's no one way to be human.

There's no rulebook that says you must connect in a specific way, or suffer if you don't.

We're all wired differently, shaped by different stories, carrying different scars.

And maybe that's not dysfunction it's adaptation.

So if your trauma taught you to seek solitude instead of connection, that's not a failure. That's intelligence. That's protection. That's your nervous system doing what it had to do.

But as you heal, remember this: you get to rewrite the script.

You get to decide what connection looks like for you.

It can be soft and slow. It can be rare and real. It can be with nature, animals, art, or a select few people who feel like home.

There is no right or wrong here.

Only what feels true.

And if you find peace in solitude, honor it.

If you find healing in quiet companionship, pursue it.

If you find God in a sunrise or wholeness in a poem, cherish it.

Because connection isn't about following the crowd it's about following your soul.

And your soul knows exactly what it needs.

CHAPTER TWELVE

THE LONE WOLF'S LEADERSHIP DILEMMA

Why Lone Wolves Resist Traditional Leadership

Leadership is often portrayed as the ultimate prize the top of the ladder everyone races to climb. But what if traditional leadership just doesn't fit everyone? For many Lone Wolves fiercely independent, deeply intuitive, and often misunderstood the typical leadership role feels less like a crown and more like a cage.

This chapter explores why Lone Wolves resist conventional leadership, what leadership truly means for them, and how to thrive by leading your own way.

The Lone Wolf's Leadership Dilemma

Picture a Lone Wolf moving through a vast, dense forest. It's not seeking solitude out of loneliness, but because its path demands it. Lone Wolves are observant, self-reliant, and deeply connected to their own inner compass but rarely interested in leading a pack in the usual sense.

Traditional leadership often means managing teams, endless meetings, and navigating bureaucracy. For a Lone Wolf, this can feel like trying to fit a wild creature into a cage made of rules and expectations.

Reason One: Lone Wolves Don't Want to Be in Charge of Others

When people imagine leadership, they picture managing, directing, evaluating, and controlling others. But Lone Wolves lead differently.

Think of leadership as a garden: The traditional leader acts as the gardener, organizing and supervising every plant's growth. The Lone Wolf, however, is like a wildflower growing naturally in the untamed woods thriving on freedom, space, and their own rhythm.

Lone Wolves are natural mentors, healers, and guides but not through top-down authority. They teach through example, empathy, and the wisdom of their journeys rather than policy manuals or checklists.

Managing others often feels like sacrificing the autonomy they value most. Many Lone Wolves would rather manage personal projects or clients than be responsible for disengaged teams.

Exercise: Reflect on your ideal leadership scenario. Is it about directing others, or leading by example in your own sphere? Write down how much autonomy matters to you.

Reason Two: Traditional Leadership Drains Energy

Leadership roles demand constant social interaction, meetings, and navigating office politics. For highly sensitive, introspective individuals, this nonstop stimulation is draining.

Imagine your energy as a rechargeable battery. Endless meetings, small talk, and managing conflicts are like devices draining your power without giving you time to recharge. For Lone Wolves, recharge comes through solitude, creativity, or nature not crowded boardrooms.

Without clear boundaries, Lone Wolves risk burnout, people-pleasing, or detaching just to survive.

Example: Someone who thrives by deep focus on creative projects but dreads meetings may find leadership roles with constant visibility exhausting.

Exercise: Track your energy levels for a week. Notice which activities drain or recharge you. Plan your schedule to protect your recharge time fiercely.

Reason Three: Leadership Demands Conformity And Lone Wolves Are Rebels

Traditional leadership molds expect extroverted, commanding, politically savvy leaders. Lone Wolves don't fit this mold.

They lead quietly, through:

- Authenticity
- Integrity
- Influence by example
- Encouraging others to find their own path

Think of the Lone Wolf as a lighthouse on a rocky shore not shouting orders, but shining a steady light, guiding ships safely without steering them.

Traditional leadership often demands conformity to a role or image, which can feel suffocating to someone who values individuality and freedom.

Exercise: List three qualities that define your authentic leadership style. How do they differ from conventional leadership ideals?

What True Leadership Means for a Lone Wolf

If leadership isn't about titles, teams, or control, what is it?

It starts with **inner authority** leading yourself fully and fearlessly.

This means:

- Trusting your intuition and decisions
- Living according to your values, even when they don't align with others'
- Embracing autonomy, even if it means walking a lonelier path
- Inspiring others through authenticity, not control or coercion

True leadership is less about wielding power over others and more about owning the power within.

Leadership Without the Title

Many Lone Wolves thrive as leaders without formal titles:

- Creators and artists leading through vision
- Thought leaders influencing ideas and culture
- Mentors guiding others one-on-one
- Innovators pioneering new ways of working and being

This leadership is subtle but powerful, rippling through communities and sparking change quietly yet profoundly.

Breaking Free from the Leadership Myth

The "Alpha" leader loud, commanding, extroverted is glorified in popular culture. But leadership comes in many forms. Lone Wolves teach us that sometimes the most impactful leaders are those who walk their own path, lead with integrity, and don't fit any mold.

The Power of Walking Your Own Path

The Lone Wolf's leadership journey is radical:

- Shift from seeking external approval to trusting your inner voice
- Move from managing others to mastering yourself
- Reject conformity to embrace authenticity
- Stop competing with others; focus on becoming your best self

It's not an easy journey it requires courage and resilience. But it leads to freedom, meaning, and true influence.

Practical Tips to Thrive as a Lone Wolf Leader

- **Set Clear Boundaries**
Protect your energy by saying no to unnecessary

meetings or social events. Your recharge time is sacred.

- **Create Solo Leadership Rituals**
  Start your day with reflection, journaling, or meditation. Connect with your inner authority regularly.
- **Find Like-Minded Allies**
  Seek other Lone Wolves or introverted leaders who respect your style. Build a support system without compromising your autonomy.
- **Lead Through Action, Not Words**
  Show leadership by what you create and how you live your values daily.
- **Practice Saying No Gracefully**
  Decline draining leadership roles or tasks without guilt. Explain your boundaries clearly and confidently.

Lead Wild, Lead True

Leadership is not one-size-fits-all. Some of the strongest leaders are Lone Wolves quiet, autonomous, and fiercely authentic.

They don't command with loud voices but guide by steady presence. They don't seek control but embody freedom.

If you're a Lone Wolf, embrace your unique leadership style. Lead your own life fiercely and authentically. Trust that this kind of leadership changes the world in ways big and small.

CHAPTER THIRTEEN

THE VOID IN EVERY LONE WOLF'S PATH

Abstinence Is Not Weakness. It's Clarity.

There is a poem by Porsha Nelson called "**There's a Hole in My Sidewalk.**" It might be short and simple, but in its simplicity, it tells the entire story of how people live, fall, and sometimes rise. In the poem, a person keeps walking down the same street, falling into the same hole. At first, they blame the hole. Then they pretend not to see it. Later, they accept they fell by habit. Eventually, they walk around it. And finally, they take a different street.

This poem is not just a metaphor. It's the story of most people's lives.

We often live on autopilot. We keep repeating the same mistakes, expecting different results. We hope that something will magically change, without us having to change anything about ourselves. But the truth is, nothing changes until we do.

The Addict's Path: Falling In, Again and Again

Let's say there's a man who walks home from work every day. On his way, he passes a beer store. He doesn't plan to go in, but somehow, he always does. He tells himself it's just one drink. But one drink turns into six. The six become a routine. The routine becomes a trap.

The first time he falls into that trap, he feels hopeless. He says it isn't his fault. The beer store was just there. He didn't mean to go in. It just happened.

But it doesn't just happen. Not forever.

The next day, he walks past it again. He pretends he doesn't see it. But his legs know where to stop. His hands know how to reach for his wallet. His mind tells him, "This is normal. You deserve this."

Eventually, he starts to see the pattern. He walks in anyway, but now he knows it's his choice. That hurts more, because now he can't lie to himself.

And one day, finally, he doesn't stop. He walks past the store. He feels the pull but doesn't answer it. He chooses differently.

And then he chooses a new route home one that doesn't pass by the beer store at all.

That's growth. That's wisdom. That's healing.

The Love Trap: The Same Hole with a New Name

Now, imagine a woman. She falls in love. At first, everything feels magical. But soon, the man becomes controlling, then hurtful. She tells herself, "It's my fault. Maybe I'm too emotional, too needy."

She leaves. Slowly. Painfully.

But then, it happens again. New man. New smile. Same red flags. She misses them this time. Or maybe, she ignores them. She tells herself, "This time it will be different."

But it's not. The hole looks different, but it goes just as deep.

After a few cycles, something clicks. She starts noticing patterns. She sees the signs sooner. She realizes this isn't about bad luck. It's about habit. It's about addiction not to love, but to chaos, to codependency, to the comfort of being needed, even if it hurts.

Eventually, she chooses herself. She stops romanticizing red flags. She avoids the familiar hole. And then, one day, she decides to walk a different street altogether.

Not because she hates men. Not because she gave up on love. But because she chose peace.

The Real Lone Wolf

The Lone Wolf is not some mysterious character from a movie. The Lone Wolf is the man or woman who finally chose not to fall into the same trap.

They are the ones who stopped walking down streets full of holes. They are the ones who chose silence over noise, solitude over chaos.

But here's the part no one talks about: the Lone Wolf pays a price.

They walk alone.

Not because they want to, but because they have to. Because they know their weaknesses too well. They know they cannot handle the old paths, the old temptations.

So, they abstain. From parties. From casual love. From the beer store. From anything that feels like the old street.

And this abstaining? It looks extreme. People might say, "Why so serious? It's just one drink. Just one date. Just one night."

But the Lone Wolf knows better. They know one becomes many. They know the hole is still there, even if it wears a new disguise.

Abstinence Is Not Weakness. It's Clarity.

It might sound strange, but abstaining from relationships is not very different from abstaining from alcohol or drugs. It's not about hate. It's about healing.

An unhealthy relationship can mess with your brain the same way a substance does. It gives you highs. Then crashes. It confuses your emotions. It disconnects you from yourself.

Every time you fall into that hole, a part of your soul gets bruised.

That's why some people choose to step away completely. Not because they fear connection. But because they're learning to connect with themselves first.

The Void Is Real

But let's not pretend it's easy.

When you stop walking down familiar streets, you start walking through the void. This is a place that feels empty. Quiet. Lonely.

You begin to miss the chaos. Not because you loved it, but because you were used to it. You miss the drama. The noise. The rush.

But slowly, something else begins to grow.

Clarity. Peace. Self-respect.

You start hearing your own thoughts clearly. You start loving the calm. You start trusting yourself.

The Final Street

One day, without realizing it, you stop checking if the old hole is still there. You stop expecting someone to pull you back. You stop needing proof that you've healed.

Because you know.

You've chosen a new street.

You don't walk faster. You don't walk with fear. You just walk free.

And that, my friend, is the real path of a Lone Wolf.

Not lonely. Not broken.

Just someone who finally stopped falling into the same hole, and chose, instead, to walk toward themselves.

The void in the Lone Wolf's path is not a punishment. It's the space required to build a new way of being. It is uncomfortable, but it is clean. And in that stillness, something powerful is born:

Self-connection.

The opposite of addiction is not just sobriety. It's connection.

And for the Lone Wolf, that connection starts within.

CHAPTER FOURTEEN

THE SPIRITUAL PATH

Alone, Not Lost

You weren't made to follow. You were made to find.

There comes a moment in every Lone Wolf's journey when the emotional storm quiets, the identity struggles settle, and the addictions lose their grip and what remains is something deeper. A hunger. A flame that never goes out. A whisper that asks:

"Is there more than this?"

And that's where the spiritual path begins not as a grand revelation, but as a quiet, aching question. It doesn't matter if you were raised religious or not. At some point, the Lone Wolf realizes that their path was never just about surviving this world it was about understanding it, seeing through the illusions, and becoming something more than what they were taught to be.

The Lone Wolf is a Seeker at heart. Not of attention, not of status but of truth.

The Seeker's Flame

For many, life is about comfort. Predictability. Belonging. But not for you. Not for the Lone Wolf.

Comfort bores you. Predictability feels like a slow death. And belonging? You've long known that fitting in often comes at the cost of authenticity.

Your path isn't paved. It's wild, unlit, sometimes treacherous but it's yours. And the further you walk it, the more you begin to realize: this isn't just a personality trait. It's a spiritual calling.

The Lone Wolf isn't avoiding the world they're trying to see beyond it. Beyond the noise, the distractions, the ego-driven systems that promise happiness but deliver only restlessness. The Lone Wolf wants something real. Something eternal.

And that's what sets this path apart: it's not about answers. It's about awakening.

Siddhartha: The Original Lone Wolf

To understand the Lone Wolf's spiritual journey, look no further than Siddhartha, the man who would become the Buddha.

He wasn't born in hardship. He had wealth, status, comfort. But none of that touched the deeper hunger inside him the call to know. To see. To wake up.

At just 29, with a wife and newborn son, Siddhartha walked away from everything. Not because he didn't care but because he cared too much to live in a lie. He cut his hair, donned the robes of an ascetic, and disappeared into the wilderness not to abandon life, but to understand it.

That moment, for many Lone Wolves, is deeply relatable. The call to step off the path society laid out. The decision to leave behind everything that looks good on paper but feels like death on the inside.

Like Siddhartha, the Lone Wolf senses that truth cannot be handed down. It must be found, through stillness, through struggle, and often through solitude.

Minimalism as a Spiritual Compass

Siddhartha gave up palaces. But in the modern world, Lone Wolves give up something different: the illusion of more.

The climb. The hustle. The brand-new everything. The endless pursuit of possessions, promotions, applause.

At some point, the Lone Wolf realizes that each new "thing" becomes a distraction from the one thing that actually matters inner clarity.

So they begin to strip it all away. The toxic job. The fake friendships. The compulsive scrolling. They pare their lives down to what's essential not because they hate the world, but because they've outgrown it.

This instinct toward simplicity is spiritual. It mirrors ascetic traditions from every corner of history. Because when the noise quiets, the soul speaks.

Abstinence, Addiction & Awakening

For many Lone Wolves, the spiritual journey also means confronting addiction not just to substances, but to people, to drama, to approval.

Like Siddhartha, who fasted and practiced extreme deprivation, many Lone Wolves go through phases of intense withdrawal. Not to punish themselves but to purify. To reclaim sovereignty over their own impulses.

It's not about perfection. It's about clarity.

Because when your life is full of cravings emotional, material, physical you can't see the truth. You can't hear your own intuition over the screaming of your ego. So you unplug. You get quiet. You observe.

You let the cravings surface, but you don't act on them. You study them. You learn what they're really hiding.

And then, one day, they start to lose their power.

Dreams, Nature & the Wisdom Beyond Words

Siddhartha didn't find truth in books. He didn't get it from a guru. His deepest realizations came from dreams... from the trees... from the earth itself.

Modern life has disconnected most people from these sources. But not the Lone Wolf.

When no one else makes sense, you turn to nature. You journal your dreams. You walk in forests and suddenly understand something that can't be explained. You sit by a river and feel time disappear. You touch a tree and feel its silence teaching you more than any TED Talk ever could.

That's not "woo-woo." That's connection. That's ancient. That's real.

The deeper into solitude you go, the louder the wisdom becomes. The world begins to whisper: This is the path. Keep going.

The Bodhi Tree Moment

At some point, every Lone Wolf reaches their version of the Bodhi tree.

A moment where you stop chasing, stop running, stop pretending. You sit down mentally, emotionally, spiritually and you refuse to move until truth finds you.

It may not look like much from the outside. You may just appear "quiet" to others. Maybe you're less social, more internal. Maybe you quit your job, moved cities, or suddenly changed your entire lifestyle.

But inside? You are undergoing a revolution.

And it's in that stillness, that radical surrender, that the shift begins. You don't need anyone to explain it. You feel it. In your bones. In your breath. In your being.

This is what awakening feels like not a lightning bolt, but a slow, beautiful burn.

Teaching Without Controlling

When Siddhartha emerged from his solitude, he didn't demand followers. He didn't start a religion. He simply shared what he'd discovered and trusted that those who were ready would understand.

That's Lone Wolf leadership.

You don't want power over people. You want to share light with those still walking through their darkness. You're not interested in titles. You're not trying to build an empire. You just want to pass the torch.

You become a living invitation a reminder that the path of truth exists, and it's walkable. But only if you're willing to walk it alone.

You Are Not Crazy. You Are Becoming.

The world may not understand you. They may see your solitude and call it sadness. Your simplicity and call it failure. Your spiritual hunger and call it madness.

Let them.

You're not here to make sense to people stuck in systems you've outgrown.

You're not lost you're becoming. You're not broken you're breaking through.

And though the path feels lonely, it is anything but empty. All around you, unseen, walk others like you. Lone Wolves. Seekers. Silent warriors. Souls who also dared to ask the hard questions.

You are part of a tribe that doesn't meet in temples or wear matching robes. Your community is invisible but it's real. It's vast. And it's growing.

Final Reflection: Trust the Pathless Path

The Lone Wolf's spiritual journey isn't linear. It's not logical. And it's definitely not easy. But it is real.

You don't need a religion to be sacred. You don't need followers to lead. You don't need permission to be divine.

Just keep walking.

Keep listening.

And remember: You're not walking away from the world. You're walking toward yourself.

CHAPTER FIFTEEN

FIND YOUR OWN TRAIL

Rebels of a Mindful Revolution

We're diving into a story that's not just about change it's about a full-on rebellion against the status quo, led by the most unlikely heroes: the Lone Wolf Empaths. These aren't your brooding, lone-ranger types skulking in the shadows. No, they're vibrant, fierce, and unapologetically carving their own paths through a world obsessed with fitting in. This is a tale of breaking free from the chains of conformity, smashing generational curses, and sparking a cultural evolution that's as thrilling as it is transformative. Ready? Let's run with the wolves.

The Lone Wolf Vibe: Not What You Think

First, let's bust some myths. A Lone Wolf Empath isn't some antisocial grump who hates people. They're not out to dominate or sneer from a high horse. Picture this: a soul so in tune with their inner fire that they don't need a crowd to feel alive. They're the ones who'll sit with you in your darkest hour, feel your pain like it's their own, and still have the guts to walk their own path. These folks see the world through a kaleidoscope of perspectives angles so unique they might as well be from another planet. And that's their superpower.

They don't follow the herd, and they don't want you tagging along like a lost puppy either. If you try, they'll flash a knowing smile and say, "Go find your own trail." It's not cold it's kind. They believe everyone's got their own epic quest. But here's the kicker: not everyone can hack the Lone Wolf life. Some scurry back to the safety of the pack, craving the comfort of the familiar. The true Lone Wolf? They'd rather face a storm alone than backtrack to a life that doesn't fit. Rejection, judgment, abandonment they've felt it all, and instead of breaking, they've turned those scars into rocket fuel.

A World Where Weird Is Wonderful

Now, let's dream big. Imagine a world where being alone isn't just okay it's the coolest thing you can do. Picture schools where kids aren't crammed into desks, memorizing formulas, but sent out to wander through forests, listening to the wind and their own wild hearts. No more "All About Me" posters to impress the teacher. Instead, kids of all ages mix it up, learning not from lectures but from the art of noticing watching, feeling, and weaving their discoveries into something uniquely theirs.

In this world, learning isn't about gold stars or report cards. It's about building a sense of self so fierce it laughs in the face of conformity. Imagine if being shy was the ultimate flex, and the loudmouths were the oddballs. What if dancing like nobody's watching was just what you *did* when music played? Picture a society where matching your friend's sneakers is weird, and chasing a desk job feels like signing up for a snooze-fest. This isn't just a new school it's a whole new vibe, where neurodiversity isn't just accepted; it's the main event.

Smashing the Pack Mentality

The Lone Wolf Empath is a straight-up cycle breaker, kicking generational curses to the curb like a boss. For too long, we've been fed a script: blend in, chase likes, compare yourself to everyone else. The pack mentality says survival means sticking together, even if it means losing yourself. But the Lone Wolf? They're done with that noise. They're not just changing the game they're rewriting the rules of human evolution.

This isn't your average "things are different now" spiel. This is evolution, baby Darwinian-level stuff. Cultural evolution means our beliefs, customs, and ways of living shift so radically that there's no going back. Think of it like upgrading from a flip phone to a quantum computer. The

Lone Wolf is already living in this upgraded reality, where self-acceptance isn't a goal it's the default setting. Words like "tolerance" or "acceptance"? They're as outdated as dial-up internet. In this world, you don't *accept* others you just *get* them, no questions asked.

The Superpower of Not Needing Approval

Here's where it gets juicy. The Lone Wolf Empath doesn't give a rip about your applause. They're not waiting for a thumbs-up from society to feel okay. Their self-acceptance is like a supernova blazing, unstoppable, and totally their own. This isn't about ditching people; it's about ditching the idea that your worth hinges on what others think. In this new world, problems like hate or inequality aren't "fixed" they don't even exist, because the evolved mind doesn't create them. They're illusions, shadows of an old way of thinking, and the Lone Wolf is already living in the light.

I'm walking this path right now, and let me tell you, it's a wild ride. No 9-to-5, barely scraping by, mostly flying solo and I'm having the time of my life. My faith in myself is like a steel trap, my calm is unshakable, and my happiness? Off the charts. I'm not just surviving; I'm *thriving* in a way that spits in the face of the old rules. And I'm not the only one. There's a whole pack of us neurodivergent rebels, cycle breakers, Lone Wolves who are rewriting what it means to be human, one bold step at a time.

The Neurodivergent Revolution Is Here

Let's talk about the real MVPs: neurodivergent folks. Those with brains that zig when others zag think autism, ADHD, or any flavor of different are the rock stars of this revolution. They've always seen the world through a lens that's a little off-kilter, and society's been quick to slap a "fix me" label on them. But here's the truth: that difference is their edge. It's what lets them break free from the herd, question the status quo, and feel the world so deeply it sparks a wildfire of change.

It's not all epic quests and victory laps, though. Many neurodivergent Lone Wolves are fighting through a fog of anxiety, depression, or fear, convinced they're broken. I've been there, stuck in that soul-crushing freeze state, feeling like I didn't belong. But then I found mindfulness not the Instagram yoga kind, but the real deal. It's about tuning into your thoughts, your vibes, your very being, without a shred of judgment. It's about strutting down your path, even when the world's yelling, "Wrong way, weirdo!"

The New Badass Survival

Forget everything you know about "survival of the fittest." The old game strength in numbers, social clout, external wins is over. The new game is mindfulness, self-reliance, and interdependence. It's about building a inner world so rich you don't *need* the crowd to feel whole. The Lone Wolf gets it. They don't go hunting for others to fill a void they've already got a universe inside them. When someone gasps, "You went alone? That's so sad," the Lone Wolf just grins and thinks, *You're missing the point. I'm free.*

This is the new survival of the fittest: thriving in a mindful, self-directed state. It's not about outrunning the pack it's about outgrowing it. The Lone Wolf doesn't rush to find their tribe, because they know their transformation is a solo gig. They're not skipping the hard stuff loneliness, grief, or pain they're wading through it, like modern-day Siddharthas, until they hit that sweet spot of pure, unfiltered being.

The Revolution Starts Now

The Lone Wolf Empath isn't some fairy-tale hero they're real, they're here, and they're shaking things up.

They're the ones daring to live differently, spitting in the face of fear and conformity. They're not better than you they're just *them*, and that's enough. The world might not be ready, but that's fine. Evolution doesn't wait for an invitation.

So, if you feel that itch to break free, to dance to your own beat, to live so mindfully it feels like a superpower don't ignore it. You might just be a Lone Wolf Empath, ready to spark a revolution. The future isn't coming it's already here, striding alone with a swagger that says, "I am enough." Join the rebellion. The world's waiting for your kind of weird.

CHAPTER SIXTEEN

THE WOLF WHO LISTENS

Trusting the Whisper of Your Wild Intuition

"Some of us don't just walk through life we absorb it."

We feel the shift in a room before anyone speaks. We sense when someone's words don't match their eyes. We carry emotions that aren't even ours like echoes we somehow caught in the wind. If this sounds familiar, then maybe just maybe you're not "too sensitive." Maybe you're just a wolf in a world built for cattle.

Let's talk about that.

Because being a highly sensitive person or what I like to call a **Sensitive Wolf** comes with its own kind of quiet power. It's not just about emotions or tears or softness. It's about awareness. Depth. Insight. It's a different way of existing one that feels everything a little more. And when you feel the world like that, it changes you.

The Weight of Sensing What Others Miss

You ever walk into a room and just *know* something's off?

Nobody says anything. No arguments. No warning signs. But still... something in the air feels tight. Like the energy shifted and your gut picked it up before your brain did.

That's not magic. That's *you*. That's your nervous system your emotional radar picking up signals other people miss. And while it can be a gift, let's not pretend it doesn't feel like a curse sometimes. You end up overwhelmed, exhausted, misunderstood. People say you're overthinking. That you need to relax.

But they don't get it. You're not trying to be dramatic you're trying to survive in a world where everyone's yelling on the outside and you're listening to whispers no one else can hear.

Where It Comes From: The Ancient Blueprint

Here's something wild scientists who studied wolves found that around 20–23% of them choose to leave the pack and travel alone. They're called dispersers. Lone wolves. And that percentage? Pretty close to the number of humans classified as *highly sensitive.*

Coincidence?

Maybe not.

Sensitivity isn't some modern "issue." It's ancient. A survival trait. Long before we had fire or language or social media, our ancestors needed to sense danger before it arrived. That flicker of intuition? That instinct that made them pause or run or hide? It saved lives.

And the ones who felt the most? Often the ones who lived the longest. Sensitivity *was* strength. We've just forgotten that.

Sensitivity Isn't Fragility It's Intelligence

People confuse sensitivity with weakness. That's the first mistake.

But think about it: If a wolf can smell danger miles away, is that weakness? If it can feel a storm coming before it forms, is that fragility?

No.

It's precision. It's evolutionary intelligence. It's the ability to *sense before you see.* That's what being a Sensitive Wolf is about.

It means your mind is tuned to pick up on undercurrents emotional ones, energetic ones. You don't just listen to words. You feel the spaces between them. That's why conversations exhaust you. Why fake people make your skin crawl. Why certain places feel heavy even when they're quiet.

But It's Not Easy, Is It?

Let's be honest this gift doesn't always feel like one.

Because when you're this sensitive, you're also this... *open*. You don't have armor. Everything comes in. You feel people's lies before they tell them. You see the sadness behind someone's smile. You carry moods that don't belong to you. And when no one else sees what you see, it's easy to think you're wrong. Or broken.

You start second-guessing yourself.

You don't trust your instincts.

You ignore the red flags because the world has told you your gut can't be right you're *too emotional.*

But that's the tragedy. When a wolf ignores its instincts, it walks into the trap it was born to avoid.

The Mistrust We Learn

Let me ask you something.

Have you ever known something wasn't right... and still went along with it? Maybe in a relationship. Maybe in a job. Maybe just a conversation. You felt it that tight knot in your chest, that uneasy stirring but you pushed it down.

Why?

Because people told you you're "too much"? Too dramatic? Too suspicious?

It's a common wound for us sensitive types. We doubt ourselves because the world doesn't reflect us. We feel alone not just physically, but emotionally. Like we're aliens watching humans perform.

It's not that we *don't* feel connection. It's that we feel *too much* of it. And not everyone else does.

So what happens? We stop trusting ourselves. We silence the voice that once protected us. And that silence... it's costly.

The Red Riding Hood Warning

Remember the story of Little Red Riding Hood?

She *knew* something was off. Her "grandmother's" voice was strange. Her hands were big. Her eyes too wide. But she ignored it. Why? Because the logic didn't match her gut.

We do that too.

We sense the danger, but we keep walking. Keep staying. Keep trusting what we *wish* were true instead of what we *know* to be true.

That's not stupidity. That's social conditioning. The pack teaches us not to trust ourselves to doubt what's unseen.

But the wolf doesn't need proof. It just *knows*. And when we learn to listen again, we reclaim a part of ourselves the world tried to bury.

The Curse of Expecting Others to Feel Like You Do

Here's another hard truth: not everyone has your depth.

They won't feel the way you do. They won't see what you see. They won't *care* like you care. And if you keep expecting them to you'll keep breaking your own heart.

It hurts. It's lonely. It feels unfair.

But once you accept that not everyone is built like you... you free yourself. You stop expecting depth from shallow waters. You stop drowning in other people's emotional immaturity. You choose peace over proving a point.

And that... is power.

From Wound to Wisdom

You've probably been burned. Betrayed. Misunderstood. Sensitive people often are. Because we give more than we should. Because we see potential in people who haven't earned it. Because we believe in what *could* be instead of what *is*.

But those wounds?

They become wisdom.

We learn who deserves access to our energy. We learn the signs of manipulation before it unfolds. We stop explaining ourselves to people who were never listening.

Pain sharpens perception.

That's how a Sensitive Wolf becomes a wise one.

Trusting Yourself Again

Here's what I want you to remember:

You were never broken. You were just tuned differently. Your compass works it's just been ignored for too long.

The world needs people like you. People who feel. People who care. People who walk away when something doesn't *feel* right, even if there's no obvious reason why.

That's not weakness.

That's courage.

So take your solitude seriously. Use it to hear your own voice again. Rebuild trust with yourself. Not everyone will understand you. That's okay. Wolves don't run with every pack they find. They wait. They wander. They watch.

And when the right pack appears one that feels *true* they'll know it.

So will you.

A Final Thought, from One Wolf to Another

You don't need to toughen up. You don't need to numb yourself to survive. You don't have to explain your sensitivity, or prove your strength.

Just keep listening.

To the air. To the silence. To the knowing in your bones.

You're not too much.

You're not broken.

You're just a wolf in a world that forgot how to hear.

And the path you're on this raw, lonely, intuitive path it's not a mistake.

It's the way home.

CHAPTER SEVENTEEN

SOLITUDE ISN'T AN ESCAPE

It's a preference. It's a love. It's a choice.

There's a word you probably haven't heard before **solophile**. And if you're reading this, there's a good chance that it might just be the word you've been waiting your whole life to discover.

A *solophile* is someone who doesn't just tolerate solitude they love it. They don't fear the silence of their own presence. They crave it. They don't see time spent alone as a punishment, a failure, or a fallback plan. For them, solitude is sanctuary. Solitude is celebration. Solitude is home.

And this, perhaps more than anything else, is what defines the **Lone Wolf**.

Aloneness Without Shame

Let's get one thing clear: being a solophile is not about isolation in the traditional, fear-driven sense. That word *isolation* has been twisted and weaponized. Society has painted it with the color of shame, using it to imply damage, dysfunction, or depression. But not all who walk alone are lost. And not all who prefer solitude are suffering.

Many of us have been shamed for enjoying our own company. Told that it's unhealthy, that we must be lonely, broken, avoidant, or even antisocial. But for the true Lone Wolf, the opposite is often true. We are deeply connected to nature, to spirit, to ourselves. We are not cut off from the world. We are simply discerning about how much of it we allow into our inner sanctum.

This life, this path of solitude, is not something that was inflicted upon us. It's not punishment. It's not the result of trauma or failure. **It's a preference. It's a love. It's a choice.**

The Lone Wolf does not retreat because they are afraid. They retreat because they are in love with silence, with self-reflection, with freedom, and with the pure, unfiltered experience of being alive without distraction.

The False Labels

Of course, this path hasn't always been easy to claim.

For many, the journey to embracing the Lone Wolf identity has been littered with the wrong labels. "Avoidant." "Emotionally unavailable." "Withdrawn." Labels that sting. Labels that don't quite fit. Maybe you've even believed them at times. Maybe you've tried to fix what was never broken.

Like many solophiles, you may have taken a course, read a book, or sat through therapy sessions trying to "overcome" your avoidant attachment style. You tried to learn how to be "better" at being in a relationship. But deep down, a quiet voice kept whispering, *I just want to be alone.* Not because you feared closeness, but because being alone made you feel more *yourself* than anything else ever could.

So what if it wasn't avoidance at all? What if it was **alignment**? What if your need for solitude wasn't a wound, but a calling?

What if your soul simply knew something that society kept trying to make you forget that your path was meant to be walked alone?

The Ache That Never Leaves

Even those who try to walk the path with another often find that something never quite sits right. It starts off hopeful. You try to give the partnership a chance. Maybe this time it will work. Maybe this person will understand your need for space, for quiet, for freedom.

But time and time again, you feel the ache. The pull. The whisper of your inner wilderness calling you back. Back to yourself. Back to the quiet forests of your own heart.

And here's the truth: that ache doesn't mean you're broken. It doesn't mean you're running away. It means you've tasted something so nourishing in your solitude that nothing else has ever compared.

If you've compromised your essence for the sake of closeness, then you know this firsthand. At some point, you realize: no amount of companionship can replace the deep, rich connection you have with yourself. And that's when you stop trying to fit in. That's when you stop labeling your truth as dysfunction. That's when you embrace what you always knew **you are a solophile.**

Secure in Solitude

One of the most profound misconceptions about those who love solitude is that they are avoidant or insecure in their attachments. But the opposite is often true. The true solophile the Lone Wolf is secure. Not just with others, but most importantly, with themselves.

Their inner world is vibrant. They are their own best friend, their own muse, their own sanctuary. This isn't narcissism. This is emotional maturity. This is the kind of self-possession that many spend a lifetime trying to reach.

Yes, the solophile may still feel loneliness from time to time we all do. But they don't fear it. They don't resist it. They sit with it, listen to it, and often transform it into something beautiful: art, insight, healing, growth.

That doesn't mean they never connect with others. Solophiles love connection just on their own terms. It's not that they reject people. It's that they no longer need to be with others to feel whole. Connection becomes a *choice*, not a compulsion.

From Disorganized to Aligned

Growing up in a world that glorifies constant connection can leave a Lone Wolf feeling out of place. The push and pull between craving connection and craving solitude can create confusion, even anxiety. At times, it may have felt like you were at war with yourself yearning for love while simultaneously suffocating under it.

But what if that inner conflict was just the result of being raised in a society that doesn't understand people like you?

Anxiety, for the solophile, can be the alarm bell that you've strayed from your truth. That you've abandoned yourself. That you've let others' needs speak louder than your own.

And healing, in this context, doesn't look like learning how to tolerate constant connection. It looks like finally admitting that your peace lives in aloneness. That your nervous system settles when the world goes quiet.

Solitude Is Not Superiority

In Professor Sam Vaknin's exploration of isolophilia, he suggested that the solophile may view themselves as superior to others more emotionally intelligent, more self-aware. And while some may lean into that belief, it's not the essence of the true Lone Wolf.

True solophiles don't choose solitude because they think they're better than others. They choose it because it's better for *them*. It's personal, not comparative. Preference, not elitism.

There's no shame in choosing yourself. And there's no hatred toward those who choose differently. The path of the Lone Wolf is not about exclusion. It's about alignment.

Becoming the Path

Being a solophile isn't about being antisocial. It's about being **pro-self**. It's about waking up every day with the knowledge that you're not lonely you're **whole**. That you're not avoiding others you're honoring yourself.

And maybe most importantly, it's about realizing that **solitude isn't an escape it's a**

destination.

So if you've ever felt like an outsider for wanting space... if you've ever second-guessed your love of silence... if you've ever apologized for needing to be alone stop.

You are not broken. You are not dysfunctional. You are not avoidant.

You are a **Lone Wolf**.

You are a **Solophile**.

And that, in itself, is a love story worth telling.

CHAPTER EIGHTEEN

BOUNDARIES FOR LONE WOLVES

From Disconnection to Self-Respect

At first glance, the Lone Wolf seems free untamed, instinct-driven, unbothered by the rules that bind others. It's easy to mistake the absence of boundaries for power. To assume that living without limits is what makes a Lone Wolf who they are.

But look closer, and you'll see something else.

A Lone Wolf without boundaries isn't free they're **adrift**. And at times, they're dangerously close to losing themselves entirely.

Because true power doesn't come from doing whatever you want. It comes from knowing **where you end and others begin**. It comes from understanding what you'll allow and what you'll walk away from. It comes from **having boundaries**, and more than that: **becoming them**.

This chapter is about that transformation the painful, necessary, beautiful process of becoming someone who no longer abandons themselves to be loved, liked, or accepted.

Born with Boundaries, Conditioned to Forget

The journey starts early. We're born with a boundary: the first, clean cut the severing of the umbilical cord. A physical symbol that we are, from this moment on, separate. Individual. Autonomous.

But then, the confusion begins.

As babies, we cry out, we scream, we signal discomfort *No, I don't want this*. But those signals are often ignored or mistranslated. A toddler says, "Don't tickle me," and an adult laughs it off. A child says, "I don't want to hug right now," and hears, "Don't be rude. Give grandma a hug."

The message is subtle but lasting: *Your body isn't yours. Your voice isn't valid. Your needs make others uncomfortable.*

And so we adapt. We soften our "no." We smile when we don't want to. We let people touch, take, dismiss, interrupt. We learn that boundaries are selfish, or inconvenient. Over time, we silence ourselves to keep the peace until eventually, we forget that peace was ever ours to begin with.

The Mask of Self-Betrayal

Without boundaries, survival becomes about performance.

We learn to wear masks confident, easy-going, chill, independent. But underneath it all, there's shame. Deep shame. The kind that whispers, *My needs are too much. I am too much.*

We become experts at pretending everything is fine. We minimize. We rationalize. We tolerate what hurts us. We people-please and shape-shift, hoping someone will finally see us and give us what we're too afraid to ask for.

And when they don't, we spiral into resentment, exhaustion, and loneliness. But even then, we rarely blame the lack of boundaries. We blame ourselves.

We think: *Maybe I'm just broken.*

You're not broken. You're boundaryless.

And it's costing you your **authenticity**.

The False Freedom of Hyper-Independence

When boundaries are violated enough times, many Lone Wolves make a drastic pivot: they go all in on **hyper-independence.**

You convince yourself you don't need anyone. That needing is weakness. That emotions are liabilities. You handle everything alone not because you want to, but because the alternative feels unsafe.

You'd rather build a fortress than risk being vulnerable again.

But that isn't strength. It's **self-abandonment in disguise.**

True freedom isn't isolation. It's interdependence. It's the ability to be *both whole and connected* not because you need others to complete you, but because connection **enhances** you.

Without boundaries, you either become a doormat or a lone island either way, you lose yourself.

Manipulation: The Shadow Strategy

When we don't feel safe asking for what we need, we find ways to get it indirectly.

We serve others so they'll feel obligated to give back. We avoid conflict at all costs, only to explode later in anger or silence. We pretend we don't care, hoping someone will prove us wrong and show up for us.

These strategies aren't evil they're survival mechanisms. They're what we do when we don't trust that we're worthy of **direct, honest, clean communication**.

But over time, these behaviors corrode the very thing we want: real connection. We end up misunderstood, disappointed, and isolated not because we're unlovable, but because we never gave anyone the chance to meet the *real* us.

Hitting the Wall: When Pretending Doesn't Work Anymore

Eventually, you hit the wall.

You wake up tired not just physically, but spiritually. You realize you've spent your life serving others while betraying yourself. You see how your silence has cost you relationships, peace, and joy. And maybe, like so many Lone Wolves, you realize:

No one is coming to save me.

That realization is devastating but it's also where everything starts to change. Because once you stop waiting for someone to give you permission, you begin to reclaim your power.

You begin the long, sacred work of **setting boundaries**.

Becoming Boundaries: The Four Steps

Setting boundaries isn't just about saying "no." It's about **reorienting your entire identity** from someone who reacts to someone who chooses.

There are four key stages in this evolution:

1. Awareness

You begin to notice where you've betrayed yourself. The moments you said "yes" but meant "no." The gut feelings you ignored. The discomfort you minimized. You stop numbing. You start listening.

2. Acknowledgment

You name what's happened without shame: *I didn't honor myself there. I abandoned myself to avoid conflict.* You stop blaming others, not because they weren't wrong but because your healing isn't their responsibility.

3. Assertion

You start practicing small, clear boundaries. Saying "I'm not okay with that" or "I need time to think" or "I'm not comfortable doing that." You say it softly at first, maybe even with guilt. But over time, you get stronger.

4. Integration

Eventually, boundaries stop being something you *do* and start being who you *are*. You no longer need to explain or justify your limits. You embody them. Your energy communicates your standards without needing confrontation. You become someone who *respects themselves so deeply*, others rise to meet you or fall away.

From Walls to Windows

A common trap in early boundary work is to build **walls** instead of creating **filters**.

Walls say, *No one gets in.* Filters say, *Only those who honor me are welcome.*

True boundaries aren't about shutting people out. They're about allowing others in **responsibly**.

Like when I had a mold issue in my basement. I could have handled it myself, quietly resenting the situation. But I chose to speak up. I said, "I'm not comfortable dealing with this," and let my landlord respond.

She took care of it. No drama. No guilt.

That's the power of **clean communication**. No manipulation. No martyrdom. Just clarity.

Codependency vs. Connection

One of the biggest shifts you'll experience on this journey is moving from **codependency to connection**.

Codependency says: *I need you to meet my needs because I can't meet them myself.*

Boundaries say: *I know how to meet my needs and I welcome others who can contribute to my life without taking it over.*

You stop needing others to validate your worth. You stop chasing love that comes with conditions. You stop performing. Instead, you show up as yourself, fully, unapologetically.

And here's the beautiful thing: **Healthy people respond to that.** They respect you more. They trust you more. Because you trust yourself.

The Final Shift: From Shame to Self-Compassion

At its core, boundary work is about **self-compassion**.

It's about learning to say, *I matter. My needs are valid. I don't have to earn love by disappearing.*

You stop blaming. You stop hiding. You start healing.

And in that process, you no longer fear being alone. Because you're no longer lonely *within yourself.* You become someone who is emotionally available to others **because you've finally become available to yourself.**

Closing Thoughts: You Are Not Too Late

If you're just beginning this journey, it's okay. It's not too late. You haven't missed your chance.

Start small. Be kind. Speak honestly. And remember: every boundary you set is a love letter to yourself.

You don't need to be louder. You don't need to be tougher. You just need to be **true**.

Because once you learn to respect yourself you'll never let anyone else decide your worth again.

CHAPTER NINETEEN

THE WAY OF THE LONE WOLF

What It Really Means to Walk Your Own Path

You see, wolves, in the wild, live in packs. They hunt together, raise their young together, move through life as a tightly woven unit. It's a beautiful, loyal kind of existence. But even among them, there are some who leave. They wander off not out of defiance, but out of something even stronger: instinct.

Scientists call it "dispersal." A lone wolf sets off to find new territory, a new life. Sometimes they travel hundreds of miles, crossing forests, rivers, entire countries. Why? Because the pack they were born into isn't where their story ends. They know there's more. And they're willing to face the unknown to find it.

That's what this chapter is about not just the wolf, but the part of you that might feel like one.

We don't talk enough about the human version of dispersal. The person who looks around at the life everyone else seems to accept and feels... disconnected. Not better. Not worse. Just different. The ones who leave jobs, cities, relationships sometimes even families not to escape, but to find a life that feels real.

It's easy to misunderstand them. People often think the lone wolf is angry, cold, or broken. But more often, they're none of those things. They're just sensitive in a world that rarely slows down. They've been through their share of rejection, yes. But what shapes them more is the resilience they've built quietly, when no one was watching.

The lone wolf doesn't need to be loud. They don't need attention. They're not trying to prove anything. Their life isn't a performance it's a practice. A practice of listening to their own truth, even when it contradicts what the world says they should be.

And they don't leave for nothing.

There's always a reason. Sometimes it's to find clarity. Sometimes it's to heal. Sometimes it's just to breathe without permission. Whatever the reason, the decision to walk away is never made lightly. It's made in quiet moments, after long nights, with a heart that's tired of pretending.

And let me say this clearly: the lone wolf isn't lonely. Not in the way people think. There's a difference between being alone and being lonely. The lone wolf values connection but only the kind that's honest, soul-deep, and energizing. Surface-level talk exhausts them. Forced relationships feel like cages. So they choose their people carefully. Sometimes that means having very few. Sometimes it means none for a while. But they're okay with that.

They'd rather wait than settle.

And while they walk alone, they grow. They learn things no one else teaches how to hold themselves through hard days, how to make peace with their own thoughts, how to trust their gut when there's no one around to confirm it.

They don't rush into anything not relationships, not careers, not decisions. They've done that before. And it hurt. So now they move slow. Intentionally. Not out of fear, but out of wisdom.

Because here's the thing: when you walk alone for long enough, you start to realize you're never really alone at all.

There's the sky. The earth. The moments of synchronicity that feel like the universe whispering, "You're exactly where you need to be." The wolf doesn't wait for the world to affirm them. They find their affirmation in the quiet. In knowing who they are, without needing anyone else to clap for it.

Sure, there are hard days. Moments where doubt creeps in. Where the path feels too long, too quiet, too uncertain. But even in those moments, the lone wolf doesn't regret leaving the pack. Because the freedom the real freedom is worth it.

And this freedom isn't just about doing what you want. It's about living in alignment with what matters to you. It's about saying no to what drains you, even when everyone else says yes. It's about choosing solitude over company that doesn't feel like home.

It's also about learning that you don't need to explain yourself. The lone wolf doesn't send out press releases about why they're different. They just are. And the people who get it, get it. The rest don't need to.

That's another kind of freedom: letting go of the need to be understood.

Not everyone is built for the lone wolf's path. And that's okay. But if you're someone who's felt like you never quite fit in, who's tired of performing for approval, who's starting to feel the pull toward something quieter, realer, more you this chapter is for you.

Maybe the lone wolf isn't just a metaphor.

Maybe it's a mirror.

Maybe you've been hearing the call too.

And maybe, just maybe, it's time to answer.

CHAPTER TWENTY

SURVIVE AND THRIVE AS A LONE WOLF

*Ten Inner Codes for Thriving Alone
in a Noisy World*

There's something magnetic about the lone wolf. That solitary figure, quiet but strong, moving through life untethered wild, watchful, independent.

But being a lone wolf isn't a trend. It's not a moody aesthetic or something you become just to sound interesting. It's a path shaped by something far deeper: the ache of not quite fitting in, the sting of emotional abandonment, the quiet decision to trust your own steps sometimes because you want to, and often because you had no other choice.

And in a country like India, where family is religion and belonging is the norm, walking alone isn't just rare it's radical.

Here, community is sacred. Togetherness is expected. Weddings, festivals, even grief everything is designed to be shared. So when someone chooses solitude, people don't just question it. They worry. They whisper. They wonder what went wrong.

But for many of us, solitude isn't a luxury. It's how we survive.

So the real question is: how do you not just survive, but *thrive* as a lone wolf in a world that demands conformity? How do you walk alone without losing your heart... or hardening it?

Here are ten quiet truths inner codes, if you will for the empowered lone wolf. Not to teach you how to be one, but to help you remember what you already know.

1. Release the Victim Story

Let's be honest: some of the pain you carry wasn't your fault. Maybe your family didn't see you. Maybe society misunderstood you. Maybe you gave love that was never returned.

But staying in that pain, wearing it like a badge, only keeps you chained to it.

You don't get to rewrite the past but you do get to choose what kind of story you tell yourself now. Are you the wounded one the world wronged... or the warrior who rose anyway?

Taking responsibility for your healing is the ultimate act of rebellion in a culture that teaches us to blame fate.

2. Be Kinder to Yourself Than the World Ever Was

If you grew up in a home echoing with comparison "Look at your cousin," "Be more like him," "Don't be too emotional" chances are, you learned to turn that criticism inward.

But here's the truth: you don't need a harsher critic. You need a softer witness.

Talk to yourself like you'd talk to a hurting child. Or an old friend from your hometown. That's what heals. That's how you grow not through shame, but through warmth.

3. Boundaries Aren't Walls They're Wisdom

In Indian homes, where everyone's lives are entangled where your decisions somehow affect your uncle's opinion and your neighbor's daughter setting boundaries feels almost sinful.

But the empowered lone wolf learns this: boundaries aren't selfish. They're sacred.

The key is flexibility. Boundaries should protect your peace, not isolate you from love. Too tight, and you cut people out. Too loose, and you lose yourself. Let them breathe. Let them evolve. Let them serve you not suffocate you.

4. Stop Explaining. Start Moving.

We've all been there explaining our dreams to people who don't get it, justifying our decisions, waiting for permission that never comes.

Lone wolves don't wait anymore. They *act*.

Don't overthink every step. Don't seek ten signs before you leap. India is full of advice-givers, but rarely do they carry your soul's compass. Trust that small inner nudge. Walk forward even if it's just a few shaky steps. That's how the path reveals itself.

5. Go Where the Noise Stops

There's a reason the sages went to the forests. Not because they hated people but because stillness speaks in ways crowds never can.

The lone wolf recharges in nature. In silence. In the sacred ordinary a banyan tree, a riverbend, the smell of wet soil after the first rain.

Find your place of quiet. Let the earth hold you when the world cannot. Let the wind remind you: you're not lost you're just listening.

6. Trust Yourself More Than Anyone Else

Many lone wolves have been betrayed. Not just by people, but by their own judgment. "Why didn't I see it coming?" "Why did I let that happen?"

So they stop trusting everyone and everything. But here's the twist: the real healing begins not when you trust others again, but when you trust *yourself* again.

Start small. Keep promises to yourself. Let your intuition lead. Your gut has wisdom your mind forgot.

When you trust your own steps, you no longer fear being alone because you know who's walking with you.

7. Redefine Power

In a country where masculinity is often mistaken for control, and silence mistaken for weakness the lone wolf redefines strength.

Power isn't about dominating the room. It's about owning your energy.

You don't need to shout to be heard. You don't need to control to feel secure. The most powerful people don't command attention they command *presence*. Their stillness speaks.

8. Don't Let Work Become Your Escape

Many lone wolves are high-achievers. Work becomes the safe zone the place where emotions don't get messy.

But overwork isn't always ambition. Sometimes, it's avoidance.

Make space for joy. For silliness. For painting with no purpose. For dancing to a song no one else likes. Play isn't childish it's what keeps you whole.

9. You're Not in a Race. Let Go of the Need to Compete.

Indian society teaches competition early. Rank first. Be the best. Settle early. Marry "right." Earn more.

But the lone wolf knows this: life isn't a ladder. It's a spiral. You keep coming back to yourself, each time deeper.

Your only real competition is the version of you that stayed afraid.

10. Speak from the Heart, Not Just the Mind

Being a lone wolf doesn't mean being emotionally shut down. It means you're more selective with your emotional energy.

So when you speak, speak honestly. Clearly. Kindly.

If you have to leave, leave with grace. If you need to say no, say it with calm. Not everything requires an explanation but everything benefits from dignity.

The Wild Freedom of Walking Alone

Being a lone wolf in a collectivist culture isn't easy. There are days it will feel like exile. Days you'll doubt your strength. Days when everyone's path looks easier than yours.

But remember this: every sacred story in this land be it a rishi, a rebel, or a wanderer began with someone stepping away from the crowd.

You're not lost. You're just walking home differently.

You don't need to prove your worth. You don't need to be louder, tougher, or more palatable.

You just need to be *true*.

So walk on. With quiet fire. With open eyes. With a heart that's been bruised but still believes.

You are not broken.

You are just *wildly whole*.

How to Be a Happy Loner

Because they weren't made to

When people hear the term "Lone Wolf," they often picture someone cold, distant, maybe even antisocial or broken. But what if I told you that the Lone Wolf is not a failure of society but the future of human evolution?

Yeah, I talk about Lone Wolves a lot. Why? Because when I started doing it, people began reaching out with the same message again and again:

"I thought I was the only one."

For the first time, someone was putting words to a deep, quiet truth they had felt their whole lives but never heard anyone else say out loud. A truth that being alone isn't always lonely. That solitude can be sacred. That preferring your own company doesn't mean something is wrong with you.

In fact, it might mean something is **very right**.

Misunderstood But Not Mistaken

Let's clear something up: The Lone Wolf isn't a grudge-holding, angry loner hiding from the world. The Lone Wolf I talk about **the true Lone Wolf is deeply kind, profoundly compassionate, and wired for introspection.**

But life hasn't been gentle with them. They've felt neglected. Betrayed. Misunderstood. Not because they were broken, but because **they were born different in a world that worships sameness.**

And now, more people are waking up to that difference. Neurodivergence, sensitivity, depth these aren't flaws. They're features of a new kind of human. A human who doesn't fit the mold because **they weren't made to.**

You're Not Broken for Wanting to Be Alone

Somewhere along the line, we got taught that being alone meant being unwanted. As kids, if we misbehaved, we were sent to our rooms alone. Alone was punishment. Alone meant isolation. Alone meant shame.

No wonder we grew up fearing it.

But imagine this instead: You grow up in a world where solitude is sacred. Where being alone is just as celebrated as being social. Where no one says, "What's wrong with you?" when you choose a quiet night over a loud crowd.

You wouldn't equate aloneness with loneliness. You wouldn't fear missing out because you'd know that **you're not missing anything important when you're with yourself**.

In fact, the people who are constantly chasing connection might be the ones missing out **on self-discovery, peace, and authenticity.**

Why Being Alone Can Actually Make You Happier

Let's be honest: some people suffered immensely during global lockdowns and social isolation. But others? Others quietly thrived. For them, it was like the world had finally slowed down to their speed.

That's the Lone Wolf.

But how do you turn that quiet life into one that's joyful and empowering? The answer isn't about becoming a hermit or rejecting all relationships. It's about **shifting your mindset from survival to sovereignty.**

Here's the truth: the Lone Wolf lifestyle isn't about rejecting people. It's about choosing **yourself** first.

You can still have relationships. You can have deep, fulfilling connections. But they might look different from what the mainstream tells you is "normal." Your needs might be met through nature, animals, creativity, or a couple of close, grounding friendships.

And that's more than enough.

The Path Is Yours Alone

Being a Lone Wolf isn't just about being alone. It's about **carving your own path** mentally, emotionally, spiritually.

It means honoring your instincts, even when they don't make sense to others. It means choosing your truth over the crowd's approval. And it means **letting go of the need to explain yourself to people who were never meant to understand you**.

Say this to yourself:

"I am a Lone Wolf. I am carving my own path. No one needs to know. No one needs to approve."

Because here's the wild thing: most people are still trying to fit in. To gain acceptance. To be validated. But the Lone Wolf already knows they're enough even if no one else sees it.

You're Not Weak. You're Wired Differently.

There's a common misunderstanding that people who choose to walk alone are broken, insecure, avoidant, or narcissistic.

Nope.

The truth is, **you've been gaslighted into thinking that choosing yourself is selfish**. That following your own instincts is dangerous. That your pain is proof something's wrong with you.

But listen: **your path isn't harmful. It's healing**. You're not here to hurt others. You're here to live your truth in a way that uplifts not only yourself but the entire human story. You lead by example. You lead by not forcing.

In fact, the Lone Wolf often becomes a beacon someone others look to in awe, not always understanding why they feel so drawn to you. It's your calm. Your presence. Your knowing.

The World Might Not Understand You And That's Okay

Even now, there are people who will mock you for being different. They'll see your independence as weakness. Your solitude as sadness. Your peace as avoidance.

But that's their limitation, not yours.

You must stop internalizing their ignorance as your truth. **You are not weak for walking alone you are brave.**

The real challenge isn't being on your own. It's rejecting the cookie-cutter paths handed to you and daring to create your own. It's turning your back on a life of fitting in and deciding, instead, to fit **yourself.**

Even Icons Felt It Like Marilyn Monroe

Marilyn Monroe is remembered for her fame and beauty, but few know just how much of a Lone Wolf she was. Despite the spotlight, she felt like an outsider her whole life misunderstood, disconnected, emotionally adrift.

Adopted. Rejected. Isolated. Her struggles weren't on the stage they were in her heart. And maybe if she'd known she was just wired differently if she had embraced the Lone Wolf inside her **her story might have ended differently**.

But this is why your journey matters.

So that others don't have to be lost in the crowd, wearing smiles that hide silent grief.

The Journey Back to Yourself

From the moment we're born, we're shaped by the energy and beliefs of others. Parents, teachers, peers, media all pouring their voices into our heads until **we forget which one is actually ours**.

But when you choose the Lone Wolf path, you begin to remember. You strip away the noise. You relearn your voice. Your dreams. Your values. Not the ones you were handed, but the ones that were always in you.

And that's the beauty of solitude. It's not emptiness. It's clarity.

Three Skills Every Lone Wolf Needs

Walking alone doesn't mean walking blindly. There are tools **essential skills** you'll need to thrive:

1. **Self-Compassion**
   This isn't about pity. It's about treating yourself with the same kindness you would give a friend. If you shame yourself, judge yourself, or belittle yourself for being different you'll stay stuck in pain. **You cannot hate yourself into happiness.**

2. **Creativity and Hobbies**
   You need things that light you up, that give your mind places to explore. Music, painting, writing, building, baking whatever feels like play. Without creative outlets, solitude becomes stale. With them, it becomes **alive**.

3. **Social Adaptability**
   Being a Lone Wolf doesn't mean being anti-social. It means being **yourself** in any room, no matter how loud the crowd gets. You learn to stand your ground, speak your truth, and connect without conforming. That's real power.

Being Alone Is Not a Problem to Solve

Most people fear solitude because they were taught to. They think something is missing. But here's the truth:

Being alone doesn't mean you're lost. It means you've stopped being led.

The Lone Wolf doesn't wander they walk with intention.

The world will tell you to get back in line. To soften your edges. To be easier to understand.

But your mission, if you're brave enough, is to **be who you are without apology**.

Not because it's easy. But because it's necessary.

The Happy Loner....

To be a happy loner isn't about locking yourself away.

It's about unlocking the parts of you that have been hidden under layers of social conditioning.

It's about reclaiming your voice, your peace, your power.

And the world may not always understand you.

But you don't need it to.

Because the Lone Wolf doesn't wait for permission to howl.

They just **howl**.

Coming Home To The Quiet Self

The lone wolf stands at the edge of the wild,
watching the young run free beneath the
moon's quiet gaze.
He does not rush to lead, nor crowd the hunt
but holds his strength ready,
a silent guardian of the pack's tomorrow.

The pack is alive, ever-changing.
Young wolves stumble and learn, their howls fresh and uncertain.
The lone wolf watches
not to control or command, but to protect and guide from a distance.
There is a power in restraint.
In knowing when to let the young hunt on their own,
to fail, to succeed, to find their strength.
Because growth cannot be forced, nor freedom stolen.
The lone wolf's eyes are sharp, always alert
ready to defend the pack if danger comes,
ready to step forward if the young need support.
But for now, the forest is theirs to explore,
their wildness theirs to own.

The Balance of Distance and Care

The lone wolf understands the balance between closeness and space.
Too near, and the young might never learn their own way.
Too far, and they might lose their way entirely.
So the wolf stays at the boundary
close enough to feel the pack's breath,
distant enough to allow the pack's heartbeat to find its own rhythm.
This is the quiet art of leadership
not through control, but through presence.

The Strength of the Silent Protector

In the stillness of the night, when shadows stretch long
and the wind carries distant howls,
the lone wolf stands tall.
Not for recognition.
Not for applause.

But because it knows its role
to carry strength for those who run ahead,
to be the steady ground beneath uncertain paws.
This strength is quiet, but fierce.
It is the strength that does not need to prove itself.
The strength that waits, watches, and protects.

The Gift of Freedom

For the pack to thrive, freedom must be given.
Freedom to run wild, to make mistakes, to learn.
Freedom to fall and rise again, to howl at the moon in their own voice.
The lone wolf guards this freedom fiercely
not by holding on tight,
but by loosening its grip just enough to let the young roam.
Because true care means trusting others to find their way.

The Wolf's Way Home

At the edge of the clearing, beneath the silver light of the moon,
the lone wolf pauses.
It breathes in the night air,
feeling the rhythm of the pack in its bones.
It knows it will never fully join the crowd
that wildness is part of its nature.
But it also knows it will never truly walk alone.
For the pack is its family, its purpose, its heart.
It watches, waits, and stands ready
a guardian in the quiet dark,
a protector of the future.

A Final Look

The young wolves run and leap,
their spirits bright with possibility.

The lone wolf smiles inwardly
not a smile of joy or pride, but of calm assurance.
They will hunt.
They will grow.
They will find their own paths.
And if ever the shadows grow too long,
if ever the night becomes too cold,
the lone wolf will be there
steady, silent, and strong
watching over the pack.
Ready to protect, ready to guide,
but never to hold back.
For this is the way of the lone wolf
to walk quietly,
to love fiercely,
and to always keep the pack safe from the edges.

Closing Whisper
And as the moonlight fades into dawn,
the lone wolf fades back into the trees
a guardian unseen,
a heart beating steady in the wild.
The pack is alive.
The pack is free.
And the lone wolf is home.

Acknowledgments

Return to the Quiet Self is the culmination of a long and deeply personal journey one shaped by the experiences, insights, and stories of many individuals who have embraced the complexities of being a lone wolf empath.

I would like to extend my heartfelt gratitude to everyone who generously shared their stories, both in person and through online platforms. Your openness and vulnerability have provided invaluable perspectives that enriched this work and brought authenticity to the exploration of solitude, empathy, and inner strength.

Thank you to the individuals from various online communities, support groups, and personal conversations who trusted me with their experiences of isolation, resilience, and healing. Your courage in speaking your truth is the foundation upon which this book stands.

I also want to acknowledge the countless authors, psychologists, philosophers, and spiritual teachers whose work informed my understanding of the lone wolf empath's inner world. Their contributions to the fields of empathy, psychology, mindfulness, and human behavior have been essential in shaping the themes and insights presented here.

Special thanks to the following influential voices and texts, which I highly recommend for further reading:

- **Brené Brown** *Daring Greatly, The Gifts of Imperfection* (Vulnerability, courage, and wholehearted living)
- **Carl Gustav Jung** Concepts of individuation and the shadow self, exploring the depths of human consciousness

- **Clarissa Pinkola Estés** *Women Who Run With the Wolves* (Archetypes, wildness, and feminine strength)
- **Thich Nhat Hanh** *The Miracle of Mindfulness, Peace Is Every Step* (Mindfulness and compassionate presence)
- **Joan Halifax** Works on empathy, compassion, and elder wisdom in human relationships

In addition, many contemporary online communities dedicated to mental health, personality awareness, and empathy have been invaluable resources. These digital spaces foster connection and understanding, bridging the gap between solitude and shared human experience.

Lastly, I wish to thank my family, friends, and mentors who supported me throughout this project with their patience, encouragement, and insight.

References

While *Return to the Quiet Self* is primarily a reflective and interpretive work based on personal insights and shared stories, the following academic and literary works contributed significantly to its conceptual framework:

- Brown, B. (2012). *Daring Greatly: How the Courage to Be Vulnerable Transforms the Way We Live, Love, Parent, and Lead.* Gotham Books.
- Estés, C. P. (1992). *Women Who Run With the Wolves: Myths and Stories of the Wild Woman Archetype.* Ballantine Books.
- Hanh, T. N. (1975). *The Miracle of Mindfulness: An Introduction to the Practice of Meditation.* Beacon Press.
- Halifax, J. (2018). *Standing at the Edge: Finding Freedom Where Fear and Courage Meet.* HarperOne.
- Jung, C. G. (1968). *The Archetypes and the Collective Unconscious.* Princeton University Press.

Additional sources include various peer-reviewed articles, essays, and interviews related to empathy, introversion, personality psychology, and emotional resilience.

Recommended Reading

Waking from the Fog

Supporting Survivors of Narcissistic Abuse

With practical tools, reflective exercises, and deeply empathetic storytelling, Waking from the Fog invites you to rediscover your inner strength and rebuild your life with clarity and confidence. Whether you're just beginning to understand narcissistic abuse or are well along your path to recovery, this book will meet you where you are and help you rise.